Papatango Theatre Company pre

The World Premiere of the winne
Papatango New Writing Prize 201

TOMCAT

by James Rushbrooke

PAPA**tango**

First performance at Southwark Playhouse, London:
Wednesday 28 October 2015

TOMCAT

by **James Rushbrooke**

Cast in order of appearance

Jessie	**Eleanor Worthington-Cox**
Tom	**Brian Doherty**
Caroline	**Diana Kent**
Charlie	**Edward Harrison**
Rachel	**Susan Stanley**

Director	**Kate Hewitt**
Designer	**Lily Arnold**
Lighting Designer	**Johanna Town**
Sound Designer	**Richard Hammarton**
Dramaturg	**George Turvey**
Producer	**Chris Foxon**
Associate Lighting Designer	**Matt Leventhall**
Associate Sound Designer	**Daffyd Gough**
Fight Director	**Tim Klotz**
Production Manager	**Ian Taylor**
Assistant Production Manager	**Will Newman**
Stage Manager	**Naomi Lee**

The action takes place in Britain, in the near future.

The performance lasts approximately 85 minutes.

There will be no interval.

Cast and Creative Team

Brian Doherty | Tom

Theatre includes *Death of a Comedian* (Soho/Abbey/Lyric Belfast); *The Father, A Steady Rain* (Theatre Royal Bath); *From Here to Eternity* (Shaftesbury); *Narratives* (Royal Court); *Famine* (Druid Theatre Co.); *Antony and Cleopatra, The Winter's Tale, Little Eagles, The Drunks, Macbeth, Julius Caesar, King Lear, Great Expectations, Macbeth* (RSC); *God in Ruins* (Soho); *Aristocrats* (National Theatre); *Stones in his Pockets* (Duke of York's); *Three Sisters, Down the Line, Translations, Tarry Flynn* (Abbey, Dublin); *The Glass Menagerie, On The Razzle, What the Butler Saw, Observe the Sons of Ulster Marching Towards the Somme* (Red Kettle); *Pentecost, Improbable Frequency, Boomtown* (Rough Magic); *Studs, Dectire* (Passion Machine); *Emma* (Storytellers); *Zoe's Play* (The Ark); *Car Show* (Corn Exchange).

Film includes *Perrier's Bounty, Garage, Bloodlines.*

Television includes *Call the Midwife, Law & Order UK, Raw, Pure Mule, Casualty, Fair City, Doctors, Glenroe, The Bombmaker, The Chief, The Wild West.*

Edward Harrison | Charlie

Theatre includes *Wolf Hall* (RSC; Winter Garden, Broadway); *Macbeth* (Park Avenue Armory, NYC); *Henry V* (Noël Coward); *The Rivals* (Theatre Royal Haymarket); *Henry IV* (Theatre Royal Bath); *The Taming of the Shrew, Cyrano* (US tours); *Time and the Conways, Joking Apart* (Nottingham Playhouse); *Sex and the Three Day Week* (Liverpool Playhouse); *Cyrano de Bergerac* (Chester Performs); *Noises Off!, The Norman Conquests, Neville's Island* (Torch Theatre); *A Midsummer Night's Dream, Much Ado About Nothing* (Lord Chamberlain's Men); *Dangerous Liaisons* and *She Stoops to Conquer* (Mappa Mundi National Tour).

On television, Edward played Adrian in *Doctor Who* Series 8 for the BBC.

Diana Kent | Caroline

Theatre includes *Long Day's Journey Into Night* (Royal Lyceum, Edinburgh); *The Heresy Of Love* (RSC); *All My Sons* (Leicester Curve Theatre); *Carousel* (Stanhope Productions); *Breaking the Silence* (Nottingham Playhouse); *Lovely and Misfit* (Fishwick Productions); *Phaedra's Love* (Barbican); *Caligula* (Donmar); *The Prisoner's Dilemma, Love in a Wood, Talk of the City* and *Roberto Zucco* (RSC); *An Inspector Calls* (National Theatre); *Arcadia* (Northampton/Salisbury Playhouse); *Venice Preserved* (Royal Exchange); *Madame de Sade* (Almeida); *Parallel Vision, Panorama* (Kings Head); *The Stick Wife, Figaro Gets Divorced* (Gate); *Les Liaisons Dangereuses* (Ambassadors); *The Secret Rapture, Of Mice & Men* (Manchester, Library).

Film includes *Suite Francaise, A Long Way Down, Turn Out, One Day, The Awakening, How To Lose Friends and Alienate People, There for Me, Brothers of the Head, Morlang, Billy Elliot, Wings of a Dove, A Kid in the Arabian Nights, Heavenly Creatures.*

Television includes *The Jesus Code, The Missing, Undeniable, Whitechapel, MI High, Switch, World Without End, The Titanic, The Jury, The Bill, Doctors, Margaret, Messiah V, Silent Witness, Death Becomes Him, Elizabeth I, Bombshell, Holby City, Midsomer Murders, Murder Squad, Ultimate Force, Nicholas Nickleby, Band of Brothers, Heartbeat, Jason and the Argonauts, Close Relations, Beggar Bride* and *Crossing the Floor.*

Susan Stanley | Rachel

Susan trained at LAMDA and most recently played the lead role of Serena in Tanya Ronder's *F*ck The Polar Bears* (Bush). She played the role of *Portia Coughlan* (Old Red Lion; nominated for Best Female Performance, Off West End Awards 2015). Other theatre credits include *The Separation* (Theatre503); *Almost Maine* (Park); *The Separation* (Project Arts Centre, Dublin); *The Last Confessions of a Scallywag* (The Mill at Sonning); *Bedbound* (The Lion and Unicorn).

Film credits include *Hotel Amenities* (winner of Best Actress, Malaga Film Festival, 2013); *Shadows in the Wind, This Chair is Not Me , The End of the Nine Till Five, Timelarks, Resurrecting the Streetwalker.*

Susan is co-founder of theatre company *Pixilated.*

Eleanor Worthington-Cox | Jessie

Eleanor was the youngest ever winner of an Olivier Award, for Best Actress in a Musical in *Matilda* (RSC and West End). Since then she has appeared as Scout in *To Kill a Mockingbird* (Regent's Park Open Air) and Blousey Brown in *Bugsy Malone* (Lyric Hammersmith). *Tomcat* will be her debut in an unshared, original creation.

Film includes Young Aurora in *Maleficent*.

TV includes *The Enfield Haunting*, *Cucumber*, *Hetty Feather*.

James Rushbrooke | Playwright

Tomcat is James's first professionally produced full-length play.

His previous credits include *Crab Bucket*, *Photo Finish* (Waterloo East), *Filibuster* (Old Vic New Voices Festival).

He is a consultant and trainer in the world of social care and also runs the Imagine Theatre School in Cirencester. He is currently on a three-year attachment with Old Vic New Voices as a writer for the Community Company.

Kate Hewitt | Director

Directing credits include *Far Away* (Young Vic); *Portrait* (Edinburgh Festival and subsequent UK tour). She has just finished working with the National Youth Theatre on their Epic Stages Project and a recent staged reading of James Fritz's *Comment is Free*, as part of the Old Vic New Voices Festival.

Kate is currently Associate Director on Sam Mendes's production of *Charlie and the Chocolate Factory* (Theatre Royal Drury Lane).

Kate won the JMK Directors Award (2014) and was the recipient of a Jerwood Assistant Director Award (2012). She trained in physical theatre at LISPA and was a performer with the National Youth Theatre and Kneehigh theatre company.

Associate Director credits include *Medea* (Headlong); *Electra* (Gate and Latitude Festival).

Assistant Director credits include *Wild Swans* (Young Vic and ART Boston); *Clybourne Park* (Royal Court and Wyndham's); *Through a Glass Darkly* (Almeida); *Breathing Irregular* (Gate).

Kate was the co-founder of You Need Me, an international theatre company, with credits including *How it Ended* (Arcola and Edinburgh Festival); *Certain Dark Things* (Tobacco Factory, Bristol and Edinburgh Festival).

Lily Arnold | Designer

Lily trained at Wimbledon College of Art.

Theatre and opera includes *So Here We Are* (HighTide/Royal Exchange); *Blake Remixed* (Little Mighty); *Things Will Never be the Same Again* (Tricycle); *The Solid Life of Sugar Water* (Graeae); *The Jew of Malta*,

King Lear, *The Taming of the Shrew*, *The Rape of Lucrece* (RSC); *Beached* (Marlowe/Soho); *The Edge of Our Bodies*, *Gruesome Playground Injuries* (Gate); *Peddling* (HighTide Festival Theatre); *Minotaur* (Polka); *World Enough and Time* (Park); *The Boss of It All* (Assembly Roxy/Soho); *A Season in the Congo*, *The Scottsboro Boys* (Young Vic, Clare Space); *Happy New* (Trafalgar Studios); *Ahasverus* (Hampstead Downstairs); *A Midsummer Night's Dream* (Cambridge Arts); *Opera Scenes* (National Opera Studio); *Red Handed* (The Place, London).

Forthcoming productions include *Up and Out Christmas Sprout* (Northern Stage); *Forget Me Not* (Bush); *Jeramee, Hartleby and Ooglemoore* (Unicorn); *The Box of Photographs* (Polka). lilyarnold.com

Johanna Town | Lighting Designer

Johanna has designed the lighting for numerous major theatre companies both in the UK and internationally, including the National Theatre, Royal Shakespeare Company, Royal Exchange Manchester, West Yorkshire Playhouse & Sheffield Theatres, as well as shows transferring to New York, Sydney and Toronto. She has worked many times in London's West End as well as at the Bush, Hampstead, Park and Theatre503, where she is an Associate Artist and for whom she lit *The Life of Stuff* (Off West End nomination for Best Lighting Designer).

She has also designed over fifty productions for the Royal Court in London, where she was Head of Lighting for seventeen years, and has enjoyed a long collaboration with Out of Joint, under the directorship of Max Stafford-Clark. Her most recent work includes *Dear Lupin* in the West End, *The Crucible* at the Royal Exchange Manchester, *Brainstorm* for the National Theatre & Islington Community Theatre and *Crush*, currently on a UK tour. She has lit many Opera productions for Scottish Opera, Trinity College Opera, Classical Opera Company, Nice Opera House, Estonia National Opera and has recently lit *Porgy and Bess* for the Danish Opera House.

Richard Hammarton | Sound Designer

Theatre includes *The Crucible* (Manchester Royal Exchange); *A Number* (Nuffield/Young Vic); *Comrade Fiasco* (Gate); *Grimm Tales 2* (Bargehouse, Oxo Tower Wharf); *Beached* (Marlowe/Soho); *Ghost from a Perfect Place* (Arcola); *The Crucible* (Old Vic); *Dealer's Choice* (Royal and Derngate); *Kingston 14* (Theatre Royal Stratford East); *Deposit, Fault Lines* (Hampstead Downstairs); *Early Days (of a Better Nation)* (Battersea Arts Centre); *Sizwe Bansi is Dead, Six Characters Looking for an Author* (Young Vic); *The Taming of the Shrew* (Shakespeare's Globe); *Brilliant Adventures, Edward II, Dr Faustus* (Royal Exchange Manchester); *Speaking in Tongues* (Duke of York's); *A Raisin in the Sun* (Lyric Hammersmith, and national tour); *The Last Summer* (Gate, Dublin); *Mudlarks* (HighTide Festival, Theatre503 and Bush); *Ghosts* (Duchess); *The Pitchfork Disney* (Arcola); *Judgement Day* (The Print Room); *Persuasion, The Constant Wife, Les Liaisons Dangereuses, Arsenic and Old Lace, The Real Thing, People at Sea* (Salisbury Playhouse); *Platform* (Old Vic Tunnels); *Pride and Prejudice* (Theatre Royal Bath and national tour); *Dealer's Choice* (Birmingham Rep); *Hello and Goodbye, Some Kind of Bliss* (Trafalgar Studios); *Breakfast with Mugabe* (Theatre Royal Bath); *Someone Who'll Watch Over Me* (Theatre

Royal Northampton); Olivier Award-winner *The Mountaintop, Inches Apart, Ship of Fools, Natural Selection, Salt Meets Wound* (Theatre503).

Television includes *Ripper Street, Agatha Christie's Marple, No Win No Fee, Sex 'N' Death, Wipeout, The Ship*.

Orchestration includes *Agatha Christie's Marple, Primeval, Dracula, Jericho, If I Had You, A History of Britain, Silent Witness, Dalziel and Pascoe, Alice Through the Looking Glass, The Nine Lives of Tomas Katz, Scenes of a Sexual Nature*.

George Turvey | Dramaturg

George Turvey co-founded Papatango Theatre Company in 2007 and became the sole Artistic Director in January 2013. He trained as an actor at the Academy of Live and Recorded Arts (ALRA) and has appeared on stage and screen throughout the UK and internationally, including playing the role of Batman in *Batman Live World Arena Tour*. Direction includes *Leopoldville* (Papatango at the Tristan Bates) and *Angel* (Papatango at the Pleasance London and Tristan Bates). As a dramaturg, he has led the development of all of Papatango's productions.

Chris Foxon | Producer

Productions for Papatango include *Coolatully* (Papatango New Writing Prize 2014, Finborough); *Unscorched* (Papatango New Writing Prize 2013, Finborough); *Pack, Everyday Maps for Everyday Use* (Papatango New Writing Prize 2012, Finborough).

Other productions include *The Transatlantic Commissions* (Old Vic); *Donkey Heart* (Old Red Lion and Trafalgar Studios); *The Fear of Breathing* (Finborough; transferred in a new production to the Akasaka Red Theatre, Tokyo); *The Keepers of Infinite Space* (Park); *Happy New* (Trafalgar Studios); *Tejas Verdes* (Edinburgh Festival) and *The Madness of George III* (Oxford Playhouse).

Matt Leventhall | Associate Lighting Designer

After serving as artistic director of the Nottingham New Theatre, Matt trained at the Royal Academy of Dramatic Art. Following time working in the Lighting Department at the National Theatre, Matt returned to RADA to become Assistant Head of Lighting.

Matt was the runner-up for the 2014 Off West End Award for Best Lighting Designer.

Matt will next design Barry Keefe's *Barbarians* at the Young Vic in November.

Theatre includes *hamlet is dead. no gravity, Ant Street* (Arcola); *Lady Anna All at Sea* (Park); *Islands* (New Diorama); *This Much* (*or an Act of Violence Towards the Institution of Marriage*) (Ovalhouse); *Scarlet* (Southwark Playhouse); *A Christmas Carol, Bear* (Old Red Lion); *After Penelope, Mrs Warren's Profession, Random* (John Gielgud); *Fishskin Trousers* (Finborough); *Collaborations* (St James); *Fresher the Musical, Wild West End, The Bear Who Paints* (Pleasance); *Tape* (Counterculture); *God's Own Country* (Edinburgh Fringe); *Divas* (Kingston Rose); *Sikes and Nancy* (Trafalgar Studios and UK tour); *Suffolk Stories* (Theatre Royal, Bury St Edmunds); *Who Framed Roger Rabbit?* (Secret Cinema, site specific); *Hamlet* (St Mary's, Nottingham);

Bedbound (Trinity, Kent); *The Infant* (Vivien Cox, Guildford); *Bed* (Nottingham Lakeside); *Madame Butterfly* (Leatherhead and UK tour); *Light* (Barbican, European tour and Bristol Old Vic); *TEDx London* (Roundhouse); *The Songs of My Life* (Garrick); *Plug in the Lead* (Leicester Square).

Theatre as Associate Lighting Designer includes *Animals* (Theatre503).

Designs at RADA include *High Society, Love for Love, In the Summerhouse, Yerma, Pieces of Eight.*

Designs for the National Student Drama Festival include *Orphans, Bluebird, This Wide Night, After The End, Proof, Talking to Terrorists, Cast Aside.*

Matt is also a regular visiting artist at LAMDA, where his designs include *Have a Nice Life, Women of Troy, But Not As We Know It, The Walworth Farce, Joseph K, The Cagebirds, Land Without Words.*

Daffyd Gough | Associate Sound Designer

Daffyd trained at Rose Bruford College.

Theatre as Sound Designer includes *Houdini* (UK tour); *A Christmas Carol with Puppets* (audiobook and tour).

Theatre as Associate Sound Designer includes *Brave New World* (UK tour; The Touring Consortium); *The Generation of Z.*

Theatre as Production Engineer includes *Invisible Dot Comedy Take Over* (West End); *Cornetto Cupidity.*

Other work includes Head of Sound for The Vaults Festival since 2014. Daffyd also has an ongoing project developing binaural stimuli designed to help Key Stage 1 children attain higher grades in creative writing.

Production Acknowledgements

Papatango New Writing Prize 2015 Reading Team |
**David Barnes, Joanna Bobin, Jonny Kelly, Justine Malone
and Deirdre O'Halloran**

Image Design | **Rebecca Maltby**

Production Photography | **Richard Davenport**

Tomcat was originally developed by Papatango with the
following cast: Rebecca Benson, Brian Doherty, Will
Featherstone, Diana Kent and Lizzy Watts.

Special thanks to Arts Council England, Backstage Trust, Dr
Nigel Blackwood, Joanna Bobin, Boris Karloff Charitable
Foundation, Professor Deborah Bowman, Derek Hill Foundation,
Garrick Charitable Foundation, Golsoncott Foundation, Harold
Hyam Wingate Foundation, Hannah Jenner, Dr Carolyn
Johnston, Iain Morris, Old Vic New Voices, May Sumbwanyambe,
Kathryn Thompson, Tricycle Theatre and Nic Wass.

THE GOLSONCOTT FOUNDATION

Papatango Theatre Company was founded in 2007 to find the best and brightest new talent in the UK with an absolute commitment to staging such work.

Papatango have produced or developed new plays in venues including Bristol Old Vic, the Tristan Bates Theatre, the Old Red Lion Theatre, the Finborough Theatre, the Pleasance London and Southwark Playhouse. Our discoveries have been produced worldwide.

The Papatango New Writing Prize was launched in 2009, guaranteeing its winner a full four-week production and publication by Nick Hern Books. The Papatango New Writing Prize is unique in UK theatre – no other annual opportunity guarantees a full production and publication.

This reflects the company's mission to champion the best new talent and launch brilliant new theatre-makers with the greatest possible impact.

2014 Prize-winner Fiona Doyle's second play *Deluge* premiered at Hampstead Theatre in spring 2015. She is currently on attachment at the National Theatre Studio.

2013 Prize-winner Luke Owen's *Unscorched* transferred to the Milano Playwriting Festival, Italy in 2015.

2012 Prize-winner *Pack* by Louise Monaghan was described by Michael Billington in the *Guardian* as 'knock[ing] spots off much of the new writing I have seen'. Louise has since produced work with Octagon Theatre Bolton and BBC Radio 4.

Tom Morton-Smith, writer of our runner-up play *Everyday Maps for Everyday Use* in the same year, saw his play *Oppenheimer* produced by the Royal Shakespeare Company and transfer to the West End in 2015.

Other Prize-winners include Dominic Mitchell, who won a BAFTA for his BBC series *In the Flesh*, having been discovered and championed by Papatango who produced *Potentials*, his debut show; and Dawn King's *Foxfinder*, which was one of the *Independent*'s Top Five Plays of the Year. This won Dawn the OffWestEnd Award for Most Promising Playwright and the inaugural National Theatre Foundation Playwright Award and won the Critics' Circle Most Promising Newcomer Award for director Blanche McIntyre. Dawn and Blanche subsequently collaborated on the critically acclaimed national tour of *Ciphers* with Out of Joint.

In 2014 Papatango established the position of Resident Playwright, funded by a BBC Theatre Fellowship and the Fenton Arts Trust. Our inaugural Resident Playwright, May Sumbwanyambe, went on to be commissioned by both National Theatre Scotland and Radio Four. In 2015 Sam Potter became our second Resident Playwright. Sam also won a bursary from the Channel 4 Playwrights' Scheme with Papatango.

Papatango run an extensive programme of free playwriting workshops in schools and community centres. All our opportunities are free and entered anonymously, encouraging the best new talent regardless of means or connections.

'Southwark Playhouse churn out arresting productions at a rate of knots' **Time Out**

Southwark Playhouse is all about telling stories and inspiring the next generation of storytellers and theatre makers. It aims to facilitate the work of new and emerging theatre practitioners from early in their creative lives to the start of their professional careers.

Through our schools work we aim to introduce local people at a young age to the possibilities of great drama and the benefits of using theatre skills to facilitate learning. Each year we engage with over 5,000 school pupils through free schools performances and long-term in school curriculum support.

Through our Young Company (YoCo), a youth-led theatre company for local people between the ages of 14–25, we aim to introduce young people to the many and varied disciplines of running a semi-professional theatre company. YoCo provides a training ground to build confidence and inspire young people towards a career in the arts.

Our theatre programme aims to facilitate and showcase the work of some of the UK's best up and coming talent with a focus on reinterpreting classic plays and contemporary plays of note. Our two atmospheric theatre spaces enable us to offer theatre artists and companies the opportunity to present their first fully realised productions. Over the past twenty-two years we have produced and presented early productions by many aspiring theatre practitioners many of whom are now enjoying flourishing careers.

What People Say...
'High-achieving, life-giving spirit' **Fiona Mountford, Evening Standard**
'The revitalised Southwark Playhouse' **Lyn Gardner, Guardian**
'I love that venue so much. It is, without doubt, one of the most exciting theatre venues in London.' **Philip Ridley, Playwright**

For more information about our forthcoming season and to book tickets visit **www.southwarkplayhouse.co.uk.** You can also support us online by joining our Facebook and Twitter pages.

TOMCAT

James Rushbrooke

Characters

JESSIE, *twelve years old*
TOM
CAROLINE
CHARLIE
RACHEL

A forward slash (/) indicates interrupted speech.

This text went to press before the end of rehearsals and so may differ slightly from the play as performed.

Scene One

JESSIE *is sitting cross-legged in the centre of the stage. She is drawing with wax crayons. She is a tiny twelve-year-old girl with long dark hair. She is expressive, playful and seemingly much younger than a normal girl of her age. She wears baggy clothes.*

TOM *enters. He is her key worker. A giant bear of a man; his giant frame entirely offset by a soft disposition and gentle voice.*

JESSIE *registers that* TOM *has arrived; she picks up one of her pictures and rips it into tiny pieces.*

TOM. That one not good enough?

JESSIE. No. (*Suddenly brightening.*) Hello, Tom.

    She crosses to him and kisses him on the cheek.

TOM. None of that.

JESSIE. What?

TOM. You *know* exactly what.

    JESSIE *laughs.*

JESSIE. Am I allowed pencils yet?

TOM. I don't think so.

JESSIE. I want pencils.

TOM. I know you do.

JESSIE. Please? Look at this…

    JESSIE *begins to move all the pieces from the floor back into a picture.*

I can't really draw with wax crayons. They don't work.

TOM. What did you draw?

JESSIE. I drew them. (*Points out towards the audience*.)

TOM. Them?

JESSIE. The people that watch.

TOM. What people?

JESSIE. The people behind the mirror.

TOM. I don't think there are people behind the mirror.

JESSIE. Shhhhh. Listen.

TOM. …

JESSIE. …

TOM. I'm…

JESSIE. Shhh.

TOM. …

JESSIE. There! If you listen carefully you can hear them breathing.

TOM. I think that might've been me.

JESSIE. It wasn't you. You breathe heavy like a dog.

TOM. Charming.

JESSIE. Wait…

TOM. …

JESSIE. They've gone now. They always go just after I hear them. Can I show you my drawings from last night before you take them away?

TOM. Sure.

JESSIE. I did one for you.

TOM. You know I'm not allowed to keep your pictures.

JESSIE reaches into her pocket and extracts a tiny piece of paper.

JESSIE. It's really small. You can keep it, can't you, Tom? Because if you can't I will rip it up. This is just for you.

TOM. I'll ask.

Lights come up to reveal CHARLIE *and* CAROLINE *standing the other side of the glass.*

CAROLINE. She's all yours from Monday. Think you can handle her?

CHARLIE. I'm nervous; to actually be in the room with her, I mean.

CAROLINE. Being a bit nervous is a good thing, hold on to that, don't let her get the upper hand; certainly not in the early stages at least.

CHARLIE. I still can't believe it's going to happen. I've read pretty much everything that's been written about her… but it's still, to talk to her… to interact.

CAROLINE (*laughing*). There she is.

CHARLIE. How has she been since your goodbye session?

CAROLINE. Unsettled. I've avoided talking about you with her. She knows someone is taking over but I wanted you to go in as a blank slate; so she can't project her anger at me leaving onto you. Tom has marked some behavioural changes in the notes. (*Pause.*) Don't watch her for too long, it gets addictive.

CHARLIE. Another half-hour max. I feel like I should get to know her, study some of the idiosyncrasies you've outlined.

CAROLINE. What time are you in on Monday?

CHARLIE. Early.

CAROLINE. Enjoy your weekend off; and try not to get too nervous. And it's not like I'm going anywhere for a few months, you've got my support.

CHARLIE. I know. Thank you.

CAROLINE. I'm sure you'll be fine.

> CAROLINE *exits*. CHARLIE *continues to stare at* JESSIE.

Scene Two

TOM *has helped* JESSIE *get ready for bed. He is brushing her hair.* JESSIE *sits and thinks for a while. She takes a breath.*

JESSIE. Can I…

TOM. No.

JESSIE. You don't know what I was going to say.

TOM. You were going to say 'can I have a dog'.

JESSIE. No I wasn't.

TOM. Yes you were.

JESSIE. How do you know?

TOM. Because it's almost bedtime and you always ask at bedtime.

JESSIE. Maybe I wasn't.

TOM. You were, and I always say no.

JESSIE. Maybe I wanted a cat.

TOM. You're not allowed pets.

JESSIE. I don't want pets.

TOM. You /

JESSIE. A cat isn't a pet.

TOM. Yes it is. Cats and dogs and /

JESSIE. Cats don't do anything you tell them. Pets have to do what you tell them.

TOM. No. A pet is any animal that you keep.

JESSIE. But they don't have to do what you say?

TOM. No.

JESSIE. But you have to give them food and make sure their house is all clean and stuff.

TOM. Yes. That's part of being a responsible pet owner.

Pause.

JESSIE. Am I a pet?

TOM. What?

JESSIE. Am I a pet? Am I your pet?

TOM. Don't be silly.

JESSIE. I'm not being silly, you have to keep me clean, and look after me and make sure that my room is nice. (*Pause.*) I'm your pet.

TOM. You are not my pet.

JESSIE. Miaow. (*Begins nudging* TOM *with her head.*)

TOM. Stop being silly.

JESSIE. Stroke me.

TOM. No.

JESSIE. Stroke me.

TOM. No. Dr Caroline has talked to you about this. Move away, please.

JESSIE. I want you to stroke me. (*Tries to climb on him.*)

TOM. Off. Now.

JESSIE. You're no fun. I was only playing. Isn't that what people do with their pets?

TOM. You were being silly.

JESSIE. If I took down my trousers and pee'd here, you would have to clean it up, wouldn't you?

TOM. No. (*Pause.*) Don't you /

JESSIE. I'm not going to. But if I did you would have to clean it up, wouldn't you? Because you're my owner and… I'm. Your. Pet.

TOM. No. You're. Not.

JESSIE. Give me three good reasons why I'm not a pet.

TOM. I'm not playing this game.

JESSIE. You can't, can you? You can't because I'm a pet.

TOM. You are not a pet.

JESSIE. Then give me three good reasons.

TOM. I'm not going to…

JESSIE (*suddenly lunging*). GIVE ME THREE REASONS.

TOM. You don't scare me. You never have, and you never will, Jessica – that sort of behaviour might work on other staff but it doesn't work on me. So be quiet and behave yourself. If you don't behave then there's very little chance that I will be able to get your pencils.

JESSIE stares at TOM intently, there is a moment. Then all malice vanishes and she returns to playful.

JESSIE. Fine, but I'm still a pet. (*Takes his hand and runs it through her hair.*) Prrrrrrrrrr. Can I show you the rest of my drawings?

TOM. Sure.

JESSIE. This one is for you.

TOM. What is it?

JESSIE. Miaow. It's a cat. This one is for you to keep.

TOM. I'm not…

JESSIE. You're not allowed to have a drawing of a cat? Even though it's my best drawing ever and I did it especially for you.

TOM. No, you know the rules.

JESSIE (*suddenly upset*). But, Tom, I worked really hard on it.

TOM. Don't be silly.

JESSIE. I wanted you to keep it so that even when you're not here, you still know I'm here.

TOM. I don't think I'd forget you.

JESSIE. Because I'm nice.

TOM. Because you're annoying.

JESSIE. Pets are annoying, aren't they?

Scene Three

CHARLIE *is getting ready for work. It is very early in the morning.* RACHEL *is infinitely more tired than he is. He is a morning person.*

CHARLIE. Have you seen my blue tie… the clip-on?

RACHEL. No.

CHARLIE. I'm sure that it was / here somewhere.

RACHEL. Can't you just wear a different one.

CHARLIE. No. I need the clip-on one.

RACHEL. Oh yeah.

CHARLIE. I'm already running late; it can't have gone far, it's a tie.

RACHEL. Shall I call you afterwards?

CHARLIE. I'm not sure what time I'll be finishing.

RACHEL. I meant I'd call you after my scan.

CHARLIE. Darling, I'm sorry. I got caught up in the excitement. Are you okay?

RACHEL. I am… I just wasn't expecting you to forget completely.

CHARLIE. I'm sorry, it's just a routine scan, I'm sure it'll all be fine.

RACHEL. It's fine. I'm fine. (*Pause.*) I am. Really.

CHARLIE. If it were any other day, I would be there like a shot. I would. It's just unfortunate that they moved it to today.

RACHEL. I know.

CHARLIE. Do you want me to try and move things around? I could still come with you /

RACHEL. No, it's fine.

CHARLIE. Call me as soon as you get out.

RACHEL. I will.

CHARLIE. You're still cross.

RACHEL. I'm not.

CHARLIE. I'll make it up to you. (*Looks at his watch.*) I'm sorry. I want to stay, I do… but I've really got to go.

RACHEL (*watching him*). Do I get a kiss?

Scene Four

CHARLIE. I'm not late, am I? We did say nine?

CAROLINE. No, you're not late. Not at all. I'm early. Bella Baker died.

CHARLIE. No!

CAROLINE. Yes. At her care home, last night.

CHARLIE. That's it then, no more Down syndrome?

CAROLINE. They want an informal presentation as it is such a landmark event, I've got about an hour to put something together.

CHARLIE. Well… it's a feather in the cap of the screening programme, they've been waiting for her to die for years. How old was she?

CAROLINE. Seventy-four. Breakfast TV this morning was calling it the 'smallpox of our generation'.

CHARLIE. Not entirely accurate…

CAROLINE. Ah-ha! Here's some material from my PhD. (*Looks.*) Some of this stuff is really old.

CHARLIE. Have you got any of her talking; I'd be keen to see it.

CAROLINE. I do. And not just her, there were three Downs people when I did my doctorate; Bella was by far the youngest, a screening error. Ahh, here she is. She was lovely. The other two were much older; Josh and his brother Dan, Josh was pushing seventy when I interviewed him, Dan wasn't far behind; they went on some of the anti-screening marches with their parents.

CHARLIE. Can you share the Bella Baker interview? I'd like to take a look when I have a moment free.

CAROLINE. Come to the presentation, I'm bringing out a lot of this PhD stuff – lots of archive interviews oh bloody hell; I forgot this… I also got the last recorded interview with Bella's mother before she died.

CHARLIE. Amazing. But I've got my meeting with Tom and then my first session with Jessie.

CAROLINE. Oh yes.

CHARLIE. I got to see her on top form after you left.

CAROLINE. She have a little explosion?

CHARLIE. Oh yeah; all superficial though. No actual real anger there. Calmed straight down.

CAROLINE. It's a behaviour that works on new staff.

CHARLIE. But she was on with Tom?

CAROLINE. Tom knew you were watching…

CHARLIE. Yes.

CAROLINE. Which means he was probably a little nervous because he doesn't know you very well. New boss, et cetera. She would've picked that up, the slightest change in his behaviour makes hers infinitely more unpredictable.

CHARLIE. Fascinating.

CAROLINE. The interviews are under my name but I've made it open-access for you; peruse at your leisure.

TOM *puts his head round the door.*

CHARLIE. Tom, you're early!

CAROLINE. I'll leave you to it.

CAROLINE *exits.*

TOM. Sorry, bye, Caroline.

CHARLIE. Come in, grab yourself a chair.

TOM. She's been really good with Jessie.

CHARLIE. Uh-huh.

TOM. I mean, she's a difficult girl to handle; but she's slowly warmed to Caroline over the last few years.

CHARLIE. I could see why you'd think that…

TOM. You don't think she has?

CHARLIE. I have a few theories and we'll come to that but I've been going over the paperwork for the last quarter.

TOM. The last quarter?

CHARLIE. January to March.

TOM. Right.

CHARLIE. There's been a massive jump in Jessie's hygiene budget. The costs this year are nowhere in line with our expenditure last year. Caroline is a wonderful psychologist but does have a tendency to sign cost sheets off without looking at them properly, but I'm a bit more… thorough. I noticed… Don't worry, you're not in trouble. I just wanted to know, why the sudden jump?

TOM. She started her periods.

CHARLIE. …

TOM. Which has meant that we've had to include more /

CHARLIE. Has she actually started her periods? Or is this…

TOM. Hannah said she has…

CHARLIE. Has it been properly verified?

TOM. What? If you mean… do I trust Hannah? Of course.

CHARLIE. Her personal-allowance budget has effectively risen by twenty-five per cent.

TOM. Sanitary products are expensive. Hannah has been bringing them in and claiming them back with receipts, I haven't managed to get a system in place yet.

CHARLIE. That won't work over the long term. Have you been recording the dates?

TOM. Dates?

CHARLIE. Of her periods; hormonal imbalances are a contributory factor in her behaviour and need to be recorded.

TOM. I informed Caroline when she started them.

CHARLIE. It's not in any of the notes /

TOM. Caroline hasn't asked us to record them so /

CHARLIE. I see.

TOM. We record what you ask and I guess that's for you to bring up with her.

CHARLIE. I suppose we should've thought about this eventuality, shouldn't we? It seems the department didn't have a plan in place.

TOM. No.

CHARLIE. I need to have a think; about whether we need to stock up with a wholesalers; or whether we stop them.

TOM. Stop them? Stop her periods?

CHARLIE. Yes. I need to speak to the hospital about the possibility of medication.

TOM. Why?

CHARLIE. Objectively, Tom, there is very little point in her menstruating; there is going to be no capacity under which she will be allowed to procreate… but, no matter – I can get on with this from here and this is a long-term option, in the short term… Get Hannah to do a costing sheet for me.

TOM. A costing sheet?

CHARLIE. Yes. So I can track the expenditure – there is a finite budget for this project. I have to account for everything in case of an audit; Caroline has let the figures get away from her somewhat. Anyway… How has she been?

TOM. She doesn't normally deal well with change but she's been fine.

CHARLIE. My introductory session with her is this afternoon. I wanted to pick your brain about how best to communicate with her.

TOM. What do you mean?

CHARLIE. You seem to have a natural rapport with her. You're not afraid of her.

TOM. There's nothing there to be afraid of.

CHARLIE. Do you not think she's dangerous?

TOM. It's not really my place to say…

CHARLIE. You're the person she connects with the most /

TOM. I'm just her key worker.

CHARLIE. Even so? You have insights into her behaviour that…

TOM. …

CHARLIE. This is all off the record. I'm not going to /

TOM. Off the record?

CHARLIE. Absolutely. I'm just interested, if I'm going to connect with her the way you do and forward the work we're doing here, then I need all the help I can get.

TOM. …

CHARLIE. It's just to get a better grasp…

TOM (*firmly*). She's like one of mine. I treat her like one of mine.

CHARLIE. One of yours /

TOM. Yes, I have a son and a daughter and Jess.

CHARLIE. So you don't think she's dangerous?

TOM. Dangerous, no. Not if she's handled properly. She's unpredictable certainly but it's not because of her brain or whatever it is you doctors seem to think; she's just messed up, confused. She thinks she's a pet.

CHARLIE. Because she's /

TOM. I know why you're keeping her here.

CHARLIE. And your advice is to treat her like a normal twelve-year-old?

TOM. Yes. (*Pause.*) And don't let her get the upper hand.

CHARLIE. You're the second person to tell me that; I'm starting to get a complex.

TOM. You'll be fine.

CHARLIE. She manipulates when she perceives a weakness.

TOM. Find me a twelve-year-old that doesn't.

CHARLIE. …

TOM. …

CHARLIE. This has been helpful.

TOM. I'm glad.

CHARLIE. I'm excited to get started; I noticed last night that she tried to sneak you a drawing.

TOM. She did.

CHARLIE. Do you still have it?

TOM. I bagged it at the end of the session. It's here.

TOM *brings out a small plastic wallet.*

CHARLIE. I'm going to allow you to keep it.

TOM. You are?

CHARLIE. Yes. I don't see any harm in you being allowed to keep it after we've taken a copy. I think it will promote a feeling of goodwill between you. There are only so many wax drawings we can keep on the file.

TOM. You may change your mind.

TOM *holds out a tiny scrap of paper.*

CHARLIE. Oh.

TOM. I…

CHARLIE. How did she do this?

TOM. I don't know.

CHARLIE. I'll ask her.

TOM. I'm not sure that'll be a good idea. She doesn't like to be caught out.

CHARLIE. Neither do I.

Scene Five

TOM *stands watching as* CHARLIE *and* JESSIE *sit drawing pictures. They don't talk, this continues for a while.*

CHARLIE. What did you draw?

JESSIE. What did you draw?

CHARLIE. I asked first.

JESSIE. I asked first.

CHARLIE. I see.

JESSIE. I see.

CHARLIE. Pneumonoultramicroscopicsilicovolcanoconiosis.

JESSIE. …

CHARLIE. You're not even going to give it a go?

JESSIE. …

CHARLIE. Suit yourself.

There is more silence. They continue to draw.

JESSIE. What does it mean?

CHARLIE. It means you've stopped copying me.

JESSIE. No. What does the long word mean?

CHARLIE. It's a disease you get from inhaling too much bad dust.

JESSIE. How do you know that?

CHARLIE. I'm a doctor.

JESSIE. Oh.

CHARLIE. Also it's the longest word in the dictionary.

JESSIE. Oh.

CHARLIE. What did you draw?

JESSIE. I drew you.

CHARLIE (*taken aback*). Me?

JESSIE. Yes. (*Pause.*) You asked me to draw what was in my head, you are here, and so you are in my head, so I drew you. What did you draw?

CHARLIE (*embarrassed*). I drew a cat.

JESSIE. You've done the face wrong, it's too round.

CHARLIE. I'm sorry. Perhaps you could show me how to draw one properly.

JESSIE. Why?

CHARLIE. It would be nice.

JESSIE. No it wouldn't.

CHARLIE. It might be.

JESSIE. You would just take it away and I would never see it again. (*Pause.*) Where is Dr Caroline? She's gone now, hasn't she?

CHARLIE. I'm sure we'll get on just as well as you did with her.

JESSIE. I doubt it. (*Pause.*) The man before Tom went too. (*To TOM.*) Didn't he?

CHARLIE. Do you miss him?

JESSIE. No. He was horrible. He used to like it when I lost my temper. He liked pushing me on the bed and into the floor and then he nearly broke my arm but I scratched him in the eyes, so he went and then they brought Tom in.

CHARLIE *looks at* TOM, *who shrugs.*

But I like Tom, because he's nice and he doesn't fight me and he doesn't push me around unless I really deserve it. Do you, Tom?

TOM. …

JESSIE. So are you my new doctor?

CHARLIE. Yes.

JESSIE. Are you going to be around as long as Tom?

CHARLIE. Maybe. Would you like that?

JESSIE. Hmmmmm. (*Pause.*) I wouldn't care.

CHARLIE. What if I promise to work on my drawing skills?

JESSIE. Are you one of the people that watch me through the mirror?

CHARLIE. What mirror?

JESSIE (*pointing*). That mirror.

CHARLIE. …

JESSIE. Are you?

CHARLIE. …

JESSIE. Fine. Don't answer.

CHARLIE. Yes.

JESSIE. What are you watching for?

CHARLIE. What are we watching for?

JESSIE. Repeating things is my game.

CHARLIE. Why do you want to know what we're watching for?

JESSIE. Am I special?

CHARLIE. Perhaps.

JESSIE. Is that why you have to keep me here?

CHARLIE. Yes.

JESSIE. Why are you keeping me here?

CHARLIE. I think perhaps we'd better have this conversation at another point.

JESSIE. Why?

CHARLIE (*ignoring her question*). I'll make arrangements for Caroline to come back and to explain more of why you're here and your history. Is there anything else you want to ask me?

JESSIE. …

CHARLIE. Is there anything /

JESSIE. I'm thinking.

CHARLIE. …

JESSIE. …

CHARLIE. Fine. Tom, mark the end of the session as 11:36.

JESSIE (*suddenly*). Can I have pencils?

CHARLIE. Pencils?

JESSIE. Yes. Colouring pencils.

CHARLIE. What for?

JESSIE. Drawing. I want to do better drawings.

CHARLIE. I'll speak to some of the other people behind the mirror and see what they say.

JESSIE. They will say no. They always say no. Don't they, Tom?

CHARLIE. I will tell them that I have decided you can have pencils; they normally listen to what I have to say.

JESSIE. So I can have pencils?

CHARLIE. I don't see why not.

There is a long pause, and then JESSIE *spontaneously hugs* CHARLIE.

TOM *moves forward ready to intervene*.

TOM (*warning*). Jess.

JESSIE (*letting go*). Sorry. (*To* CHARLIE.) I'm not supposed to grab people and make sudden movements. Sorry sorry sorry sorry.

TOM. Come on, missy…

Scene Six

CAROLINE. How did it go?

CHARLIE. Great first session. Made a really positive start with her.

CAROLINE. How was she?

CHARLIE. She was fine… we had an… interesting time. She spent the first forty minutes in complete silence, just glaring at me. Then we spoke a little bit…

CAROLINE. You can ride out the silent treatment; did she repeat your words back?

CHARLIE. Yes.

CAROLINE. Annoying, isn't it?

CHARLIE. Yes.

CAROLINE. Did you rise to it?

CHARLIE. Of course not.

CAROLINE. Good.

CHARLIE. I have a question though.

CAROLINE. Yes?

CHARLIE. She's completely unaware of why she's being kept under observation. I double-checked the notes back last night, at no point since she has been here have you attempted to explain things to her. What was your rationale for that?

CAROLINE. We never thought it prudent.

CHARLIE. Not prudent? She has no idea at all.

CAROLINE. There were a number of discussions between myself and other professionals that weren't reflected in the notes.

CHARLIE. Weren't reflected?

CAROLINE. No.

CHARLIE. Then how are future teams supposed to know how and why you've made the decisions you have.

CAROLINE. I understand where you're coming from but we have our reasons.

CHARLIE. I want to tell her; at least in part.

CAROLINE. …

CHARLIE. I don't see the need for secrecy.

CAROLINE. You won't remember Dr Beckwith, she co-authored some of the first papers about Jessie; but her primary focus was studying the effect of labelling on mental illness.

CHARLIE. I've read Beckwith's work but it's not applicable because Jessie isn't mentally ill. All the evidence points to the presence of /

CAROLINE. I know what the evidence suggests, hell I authored most of it…

CHARLIE. Which makes no sense, she has no frame of reference for any label.

CAROLINE. It was believed she would create non-cooperative behaviours and *attribute* them to her diagn– /

CHARLIE. Attribute them? How? She doesn't have an understanding of her diagnosis.

CAROLINE. I didn't see any reason to go against the recommendations. Custody was granted to us after her mother's suicide, under a certain number of conditions.

CHARLIE. Yes I know.

CAROLINE. But this is important; I'm trying to explain; that Jessie must pose no risk of significant harm to members of the general public and that in working with her we can absolutely guarantee the safety of all staff and must take reasonable precautions to ensure her behaviour is controlled.

CHARLIE. Exactly. And it is.

CAROLINE. When she was six we told her a little bit about her past. She made a spirited bid for freedom; rushed the door during a changeover. She was restrained by two members of staff, one of whom received a scratch to his retina.

CHARLIE. Because the staff members weren't adequately trained in restraint technique?

CAROLINE. That was the defence we used; we defended it by blaming the shortcomings of the recruitment process, then we brought Tom in.

CHARLIE. And that worked?

CAROLINE. It changed the whole direction of the project. She's still here, isn't she?

CHARLIE. ...

CAROLINE. They put her on a Contingent Destruction Order. A final warning. If we can't guarantee the safety of our staff under all circumstances then... well... you've read the rest.

CHARLIE. …

CAROLINE. Since that time, we've primarily focused on observation.

CHARLIE. To what end?

CAROLINE. What do you mean?

CHARLIE. We're supposed to be testing her. Aren't we?

CAROLINE. Yes.

CHARLIE. Then surely observation alone is not enough. Was any analysis done on the attack where she tried to escape?

CAROLINE. She deliberately targeted the eyes of one of the staff at the point of restraint.

CHARLIE. That's not in the notes.

CAROLINE. No, it's not. (*Pause*.) We were in danger of losing her; we hadn't completed the studies.

CHARLIE. But you haven't progressed since that point…

CAROLINE. *She* has progressed a huge amount. We've done a large number of observations, we've given her the Stroop test; she thought it was fun.

CHARLIE. …

CAROLINE. …

CHARLIE. I've agreed to give her pencils. Colouring pencils.

CAROLINE. How can you guarantee she won't hurt anyone?

CHARLIE. I can't. But isn't that the point. Any observable evidence of intention to harm would be a sign, we would *have* something.

CAROLINE. But…

CHARLIE. She's under twenty-four-hour surveillance; we may not be able to predict spontaneous violent outbursts, but we will be able to spot signs of premeditated violence. (*Pause*.) I want to run more tests.

CAROLINE. Tests?

CHARLIE. What is it? Four of them? Four that we know of, and the other three are all over the age of thirty. It's completely new territory. We have a duty to /

CAROLINE. We also have a duty of care.

CHARLIE. We have a once-in-a-lifetime chance to study the development of psychopathy whilst the teenage brain undergoes myelination.

CAROLINE. Yes.

CHARLIE. You read my doctoral thesis?

CAROLINE. About halfway through, it's my bedtime reading.

CHARLIE. Convinced?

CAROLINE. You raise some interesting theories.

CHARLIE. Theories at the moment perhaps, but Jessie represents our best chance of being able to prove for certain /

CAROLINE. I'm sure once you get to know her that you'll find her much more complex than specific hemispheric defects; your theory doesn't account for brain regrowth in the /

CHARLIE. Keep reading. Towards the end I address the ability of psychopaths to mimic complex emotional relationships and manipulate to cover their brain dysfunction.

CAROLINE. Interesting. You don't think there will be any reconnection of her neural pathways.

CHARLIE. I want to start scanning her brain.

CAROLINE. She has a strong phobia of MRI scanners.

CHARLIE. A documented one?

CAROLINE. We ran a lot of tests when she was younger; it upset her greatly.

CHARLIE. And this phobia has transferred across into early adolescence?

CAROLINE. We haven't pushed /

CHARLIE. She might have faked the phobia.

CAROLINE. We have observations. She gets anxious when we talk about medical testing.

CHARLIE. Does she? Or does she just appear anxious?

CAROLINE. …

CHARLIE. Your notes all seem to be leading us towards the conclusion that her latent psychopathy is what it appears, latent. I presume you've been working towards a hypothesis that brain restructuring during puberty will cancel the genetic imperative.

CAROLINE. Broadly speaking, yes. Her behaviour at the moment is what is expected of most pubescent children in her demographic. Admittedly she does have some aspects of conduct disorder; but she's also been kept in isolation and that would result in a whole spectrum of behaviours that would set her apart from normal development. She fits into the bell curve. She's normal. The genetic traits are there undoubtedly, but I believe we have a window of opportunity in which to rewrite the /

CHARLIE. Rubbish. The absence of evidence is not evidence of absence. You're just inferring limited pro-social emotionality to build the case against /

CAROLINE. She's a teenage girl, Charlie.

CHARLIE. And you're still treating her exactly as you did when she was six. Infantilising her. I told her that we'd tell her why she was in here; I told her that you would come back and explain things to her.

CAROLINE. Why? I've done a full debrief, said my goodbyes. Do you know how potentially disruptive that could be?

CHARLIE. You're the only member of staff who directly worked with her mum.

CAROLINE. I know.

CHARLIE. You can provide additional information that the rest of us don't know. Please, Caroline? I've weighed it up and it's better for Jessie that it comes from you.

Pause.

CAROLINE. Okay.

CHARLIE. Thank you.

CAROLINE. You should go home. This place will eat your life.

CHARLIE. I'm going soon.

CAROLINE. You have a lovely wife to get back to.

CHARLIE. I'm going to do one last observation write-up, then head home. See you tomorrow.

Scene Seven

Lights come up to reveal JESSIE *and* TOM. *She is having her hair done ready for bed.*

TOM. Have you brushed your teeth?

JESSIE. Yes.

TOM. Let me see.

JESSIE *shows her teeth.*

Good girl.

JESSIE. Are you going to read me a story?

TOM. You're old enough to read your own story.

JESSIE. Awwww. (*Pause.*) Will that other man be back?

TOM. Probably.

JESSIE. I liked him.

TOM. Did you?

JESSIE. Yes.

TOM. I'm sure he'll be back. Do you want anything else?

JESSIE. Goodnight kisses. (*Points at her lips*.)

TOM. Don't be silly.

JESSIE. Awww. (*Points at her head*.)

> TOM *kisses his hand. She does the same. They high five*.

Thanks. (*Pause*.) Can I draw for a bit?

TOM. Yes. But lights out in ten minutes…

JESSIE. Okay.

TOM. …

JESSIE. What?

TOM. You're being very good tonight. What are you up to?

JESSIE. Nothing.

TOM. …

JESSIE. …

TOM. What are you up to?

JESSIE. Nothing. Just want my pencils.

TOM. Oh, I see.

JESSIE. If I'm good, I get my pencils.

TOM. Apparently so.

JESSIE. So I'm being good. And you like it when I'm good.

TOM. Yes I do.

JESSIE. Tom?

TOM. Yes?

JESSIE. Can you tell me about the other people behind the mirror?

TOM. No.

JESSIE. Are they nice people?

TOM. I think so.

JESSIE. Are they scared of me?

TOM. I don't know. Maybe.

JESSIE. Are you scared of me?

TOM. No. Go to sleep. I'll see you in the morning. I'm on an early.

JESSIE. I'm not scared of you either. I'm not scared of anything.

TOM. Goodnight.

JESSIE. Goodnight.

> TOM *leaves*.

Scene Eight

RACHEL *is at home*. CHARLIE *enters*.

CHARLIE. Any news yet?

RACHEL. Not yet.

CHARLIE. Definitely coming tonight?

RACHEL. That's what they said.

CHARLIE. How was it?

RACHEL. I was in and out within half an hour, the nurse was very nice. How was your day?

CHARLIE. Good, it's an amazing project to be involved with.

RACHEL. Did you finally get to meet her?

CHARLIE. I did some work with her, we drew pictures. Hers were considerably better than mine. Then I screwed up a bit, agreed that I would tell her why she's in an observation unit, she didn't know. Had a bit of a tricky moment with Caroline.

RACHEL. Oh?

CHARLIE. She didn't think I'd thought through how I was going to tell a twelve-year-old girl she's a psychopath.

RACHEL. And have you?

CHARLIE. Not yet.

RACHEL. Tell me what she's like. Is she scary?

CHARLIE. Not even a little bit.

RACHEL. Not at all?

CHARLIE. No. She looks exactly like a normal twelve-year-old girl.

RACHEL. That's even more scary. I mean… how would you know?

CHARLIE. You wouldn't. (*Pause*.) Oh… let me show you.

He brings out a photocopy of a very impressive line-drawing of TOM.

Look at this. Would you give her a place in your art class?

RACHEL. She's good… some of the perspective is off.

CHARLIE. That's not the best bit. This one is a copy; blown up. She did it as a secret art project for Tom, that's him in the picture.

RACHEL. That's sweet. Creepy but sweet.

CHARLIE. She did this on a piece of paper the size of a postage stamp; with a bristle from her hairbrush, and blood from her finger.

RACHEL. That's disgusting.

CHARLIE (*excitedly*). We had no idea she was so artistic, she's only been allowed wax crayons, for obvious reasons. This is a massive development in our understanding of her nature and how she might express herself. She knows her drawings are all taken for analysis, she's working specifically on Tom, that's her key worker, as part of a long-term plan to ensure she gets the things that she wants. She's noticed she tends to get requests granted when Tom asks for /

RACHEL *snores*.

Sorry, I got carried away.

RACHEL. Take the drawing away, it's making me feel sick.

CHARLIE. I thought you said it was good?

RACHEL. Until I found out it was done in blood. Disgusting. Pack it away.

CHARLIE. This one isn't done in blood, this one is a copy. The blood one is in her file. I thought you'd be interested, it's art after all.

There is a small pipping sound.

What was that? Is it them?

RACHEL. Yes.

CHARLIE. Open it.

RACHEL. I am.

CHARLIE sinks into the chair. RACHEL *begins to cry. They cuddle.*

The lights come up on JESSIE. *She wakes up slowly. She finds a packet of pencils at the end of her bed. She doesn't know how they got there. There is a moment of magic.*

Scene Nine

CAROLINE. Good morning.

CHARLIE. I ordered that some pencils be dropped in for her last night. Want to see?

CAROLINE. Already?

CHARLIE. Yeah. Have a look on camera four. She's been doing that since she got up.

CAROLINE. Has she seen any workers?

CHARLIE. No. I want to see what she does when she's left alone for a while.

CAROLINE. What is she drawing?

CHARLIE. It's hard to tell. For a while she was looking out of the skylight. Then she moved, and I can't get a good angle. I wondered if she's doing it deliberately.

CAROLINE. She does know where the cameras are, but she doesn't know the field of vision for them all.

CHARLIE. Could she have worked it out?

CAROLINE. I doubt it.

CHARLIE. I'll ask to see them when we go in.

CAROLINE. You still want us to tell her?

CHARLIE. Absolutely.

TOM *enters*.

Tom. Come in, come in. Thanks for dropping in.

TOM. I got your message.

CHARLIE. I wanted to see you before you went in. She's awake.

TOM. Is she?

CHARLIE. Yes.

TOM. That's early for her.

CHARLIE. I had them feed birdsong into her room a little louder. Craig was on the night shift and I asked him to leave pencils on the end of her bed during the night.

TOM. Pencils?

CHARLIE. Colouring pencils. Look.

TOM *looks at the screen.*

She seems very happy. Wouldn't you say?

TOM. She would be, she's been asking for pencils for a long time.

CHARLIE. Yes.

TOM. I was told that they would be too dangerous.

CHARLIE. They won't be, given proper management. I wanted to make you aware that today we're going to be telling her a bit about her history.

TOM. Right…

CHARLIE. It's likely to be edgy. I can call in extra support if you'd like.

TOM. Why didn't you wait until afterwards?

CHARLIE. To give her the pencils?

TOM. Yes. Doesn't make much sense to me.

CHARLIE. I have given her the capacity for violence; but conversely I have pushed her endorphin levels through the roof. In short… she's very happy. At the moment she is content; what we're going to tell her is likely to upset her, given the track record of conversations about her mother *but* this is the best chance we have to measure the full range of emotional swing.

TOM. And if it goes wrong?

CHARLIE. It won't; that's why I'm telling you now. I don't want things to go wrong.

TOM. Right.

CHARLIE. And I want you to go and speak to her as you normally would; and keep her in this good mood. Caroline and I will be in at half-ten. You can sign out some sedatives.

TOM *and* CAROLINE *make eye contact.*

CAROLINE. We haven't needed to sedate her for over three years...

CHARLIE. I'm aware of that.

TOM. Are you sure that /

CHARLIE. If you're unhappy about the level of restraint you can provide, I can call Craig or Hannah.

TOM. That won't be necessary, I need to get back to the unit.

TOM *exits.*

Pause.

CAROLINE. Everything okay, Charlie?

CHARLIE. Fine. (*Pause.*) Yes. Sorry... I'm a bit... we've had some bad news.

CAROLINE. Oh... I'm so sorry.

CHARLIE. Three-month scan and it's negative... cystic fibrosis.

CAROLINE. Is your wife okay?

CHARLIE. She'll be fine... Thank you. I think we should talk about how we're going to handle Jessie.

CAROLINE. Agreed.

Scene Ten

JESSIE. Hi, Tom.

TOM. How did you know it was me?

JESSIE. Your walk, it's boom, gap, boom, gap, boom. Hannah goes boom, boom, boom, like she's running everywhere.

TOM. I see. What are you doing?

JESSIE. Drawing. I got pencils.

TOM. So I can see.

JESSIE. Did you bring them?

TOM. No. I wasn't working last night.

JESSIE. Was it the new doctor?

TOM. Yes.

JESSIE. Good. I like him.

TOM. Because he gave you pencils?

JESSIE. Yes. He's nice, isn't he?

TOM. What are you drawing?

JESSIE. I'm drawing the bird.

TOM. Which bird?

JESSIE. The bird isn't there any more, but it was there, so I took a photograph in my head and now I'm drawing where the bird was.

TOM. What bird was this? Come here. Let me brush your hair. You look like you've been dragged backwards through a hedge. Come over here and let me sort you out before the doctors arrive to talk to you. Tell me about the bird.

JESSIE *obediently comes and sits by him.*

JESSIE. It was a big bird. There were lots of little birds near the skylight and then there was a big bird that came down...

TOM. Right.

JESSIE. And when the big bird flew down all the other ones ran off, well… Not ran off, they flew off because they're birds. And this bird had a funny thing round its leg. It was a bigger bird.

TOM. It was probably a hawk.

JESSIE. A hawk?

TOM. Remember last week, when we were looking up. I pointed at that bird that was doing circles in the sky.

JESSIE. Yes.

TOM. That was a hawk.

JESSIE. Was it the same one?

TOM. It might've been, there aren't many of them and they tend to be on their own.

JESSIE. He was up so high.

TOM. Yes he was.

JESSIE. But when he came down he was really big and beautiful.

TOM. And dangerous.

JESSIE. I wasn't scared of him.

TOM. He's not dangerous for us, but he's a bird of prey. He's dangerous for other birds.

JESSIE. His feathers were so many different colours. I can't get all the colours on my pencil. What's a bird of prey?

TOM. Means that he sometimes kills and eats other birds.

JESSIE. Does he? That's scary. That's why they flew off!

TOM. Exactly. Next time he comes you have a look at how sharp his beak is. Scary.

JESSIE. Only scary for other birds though. Not for us.

TOM. No. Not for us. Can I see your drawing?

JESSIE *hands him her drawing.*

This is really good.

JESSIE. Thanks. You can have it if you want, when it's finished.

TOM. I'll have to give it in.

JESSIE. I will ask Dr Charlie if you can keep things I give you. He will say yes. He likes me.

TOM. Does he?

JESSIE. Yes. (*Pause.*) Tom?

TOM. You can't have one.

JESSIE. What?

TOM. A hawk. You can't have one. They're a protected species. I can tell what you're going to ask.

JESSIE. I don't want one; it would be cruel cos it would forget it could fly, but we could build a place for the birds to sit near the top window, couldn't we? So I could draw them. That would be nice, wouldn't it?

TOM (*brightly*). I don't see why not?

The buzzer sounds. CHARLIE *enters, followed by* CAROLINE.

CHARLIE. Hello, Jessie.

JESSIE (*brightly*). Hello. (*Spotting* CAROLINE.) Why is Dr Caroline back?

CHARLIE. I wanted you to see Professor Harper one last time. She's here to answer your questions.

JESSIE. I don't have any questions.

CHARLIE. About your parents… about your mum in particular.

JESSIE. I don't have a mum, she's dead. (*To* CHARLIE.) Why can't *you* answer my questions? You're my doctor now.

CHARLIE. I can answer some; but not all of them.

JESSIE. You're supposed to be smart.

CAROLINE *has moved across to look at the drawing*.

Don't touch that.

CAROLINE. This is very good, did you draw this?

JESSIE. I said don't touch it. It's not yours. You never let me have pencils so you don't get to look at my drawings.

CHARLIE. I've brought Professor Harper here so that she can answer the questions that you have. We both agreed that it was important / for your…

JESSIE. I didn't agree.

CAROLINE. Your mother was a very good artist.

JESSIE. I said 'I DIDN'T AGREE'.

JESSIE stares at her. TOM attempts to move the pencils out of reach.

CHARLIE. Leave them.

TOM *looks at* CAROLINE, *who nods*.

JESSIE. …

CHARLIE. Professor Harper and I were talking about your drawing.

JESSIE. I don't want to know.

CAROLINE. Your mother was homeless and so she would occasionally draw people for money, whenever she could get hold of the paper and something to draw with. She was very proficient. She had a good eye.

CHARLIE. Jessie?

JESSIE. So?

CAROLINE. Artistic ability is a genetic trait, passed down from parents to their children. You're creative because of the way that your brain is structured, same as your mum.

JESSIE. …

CAROLINE. I think you've got your drawing skills from her. Nobody has ever taught you how to draw or paint; you just have the right sort of hand-to-eye coordination.

JESSIE. …

TOM. I can't do it. It isn't easy for me, is it?

JESSIE. I can. It's easy for me.

CAROLINE. I've come here to talk to you about your mother. If you feel like you want to talk and you're ready.

JESSIE. …

CHARLIE. Unfortunately, Jessica, Professor Harper is a very busy lady with lots of important things to do; so I'm only going to give you one minute to ask any questions.

CAROLINE. Charlie…

CHARLIE. After that, she won't be back at all. Today is your only chance, after today there won't be anyone left who knew your mother. So if you don't want to talk to her, that's fine. You have sixty seconds.

CAROLINE. Charlie… I'm not sure.

JESSIE. I think she's a witch.

CHARLIE. That's fine, but if you want to have a *grown-up* conversation with someone about your mother then this is your only chance. Fifty seconds left.

JESSIE. I think you're a witch.

CAROLINE (*calmly*). I'm sure.

CHARLIE. Think about this carefully, Jessica, because this is your one chance. I didn't know your mother…

JESSIE *takes up her pencils and begins drawing.*

CAROLINE *goes to say something.* CHARLIE *waves her into silence.*

CHARLIE *waits between* CAROLINE *and* JESSIE, *entranced.* CAROLINE *continually shoots him worried glances, which he chooses to ignore.*

You have thirty seconds left.

JESSIE. I'm busy. Be quiet.

JESSIE *is becoming more agitated. She keeps looking over at* CAROLINE, *who stares impassively back at her.*

CHARLIE. Twenty seconds left.

JESSIE *throws her pencils across the room. She holds one.*

TOM *makes to restrain her,* CHARLIE *indicates that he shouldn't.* JESSIE *makes a dart towards* CAROLINE, *who doesn't flinch.* JESSIE *breaks the pencil in half in frustration.*

CHARLIE *smiles.*

Ten seconds left.

JESSIE (*to* TOM). Make him stop counting.

JESSIE *is angry now and pacing.* CHARLIE *begins to count down.*

CHARLIE. Ten.

JESSIE. Tom, I don't like it.

CHARLIE. Nine.

JESSIE. Stop counting.

CHARLIE. Eight.

JESSIE. I said stop counting.

CHARLIE. Seven.

JESSIE. …

CHARLIE. Six.

JESSIE. She's a stupid witch and I hate her.

CHARLIE. You've said. Five.

JESSIE (*upset*). Why are you still counting?

CHARLIE. Because. Four.

JESSIE. I don't like it. Tom, I don't like it.

CHARLIE. That doesn't matter. Three.

JESSIE. Please don't.

CHARLIE. Two.

JESSIE. This isn't fair. Tom, make him stop.

CHARLIE. One.

JESSIE. Stop counting! I want to know.

There is a long silence.

CAROLINE. What would you like to know?

JESSIE. Do I look like her?

CAROLINE. Very much so. She had green eyes like you and you will grow up to look a lot like her.

JESSIE. Can I have a picture of her?

CAROLINE. That is for Dr Mitchell to decide.

JESSIE. And she could draw?

CAROLINE. Yes. She was very good.

JESSIE. Did she want to see me?

CAROLINE. She always wanted to see you.

JESSIE. She left me here.

CAROLINE. She had to.

JESSIE. Why?

CAROLINE. Because she was forced to; you were two by the time we found you. You won't remember, but you lived on the streets together, you and your mum, you moved around a lot.

You were what we call 'Fades', people who have chosen not to be part of our society. They hide a lot. Your mother was hiding.

JESSIE. Why?

CAROLINE. She had a type of illness, which she got from her mother and father – and they belonged to a group of people who did not want their children to be scanned.

JESSIE. Why?

CAROLINE. They didn't like the idea of everyone knowing everything about them.

JESSIE. So. I don't like everyone knowing everything about me, but they do.

CAROLINE. And your mum was scared if they found out about what was happening in her brain that you would be taken from her.

JESSIE. And you did.

CAROLINE. She was very sick when you came to us.

JESSIE. Why?

CAROLINE. She had voices in her head.

JESSIE. What's wrong with having voices in your head? I have voices in my head; I bet you have voices in your head. When I remember things that Tom has said, I have Tom's voice in my head. Everyone has voices.

CHARLIE. Your mum's voices were bad voices.

JESSIE. …

CAROLINE. The voices told her to do things and she would drink alcohol and take drugs to make the voices go away, but if she did that then she couldn't look after you properly.

JESSIE. I bet she could have. You just didn't let her because you're a witch.

CAROLINE. The voices in her head told her that she had to stab someone, and she did. She stabbed a man and she was

arrested and put in a cell. Eventually she calmed down
enough to tell us that she had a little baby girl and where you
were and we picked you up. You were asleep at the time.

JESSIE. *You* brought me here.

CAROLINE. After a lot of arguing in the courts, yes; Dr
Mitchell will show you the newspaper clippings. Your
mother was very determined to get you back.

JESSIE. But she didn't.

CAROLINE. It was impossible… but she never stopped
fighting.

JESSIE. You met her?

CAROLINE. Yes, many times. I was leading the research into
your genetic background.

JESSIE. What was she like?

CAROLINE. She was about my height, maybe a bit smaller
than /

JESSIE. Not what did she look like. What was she like?

CAROLINE. What do you mean?

JESSIE. Like me, I'm a cat… because I'm Tom's pet, even if he
doesn't admit it. I do my own thing because that's what cats
do, and everyone likes me and gives me treats. I'm a cat.
What was she?

CAROLINE (*with feeling*). She was a very beautiful lady, and
fragile, and so very delicate; but hard underneath with a
strong mind, and very clever to avoid being caught for so
long.

JESSIE. She sounds like a leopard, because they are beautiful
and they are good at running. She is like a big cat and I am
like a little cat.

CAROLINE. In a way, yes.

JESSIE. How did she die?

CAROLINE (*looking at* CHARLIE). This may be something for you to talk to Dr Mitchell about. There are letters and other things that Dr Mitchell, that Charlie will share with you when he feels you are ready.

JESSIE. I'm ready now.

CHARLIE. That's my decision to make.

CAROLINE. Perhaps we should put an end to this session.

JESSIE. Was it *you* that put me in here and sent her away.

CAROLINE. …

JESSIE. They built this house? Just for me. And you've been watching me?

CAROLINE. Yes, in a way.

JESSIE. What are you looking for? Why didn't you just ask me? I would've told you.

CAROLINE. You're a psychopath; we don't have any of those types of people any more – at least not ones that we know about. You have the right genetic markers, the bits inside you that make you you. They all say that you're a psychopath but we're watching to see what might happen in your brain as you grow up. There aren't very many psychopaths left in the world and you're the only one that we know of who is your age.

JESSIE. What does a psychopath do?

CAROLINE. Lots of things. It's complicated /

JESSIE. I've been good!

CHARLIE. Recently you have been.

JESSIE. How good do I have to be?

CAROLINE. It's not as simple as that. You just keep being you and we will keep writing things down.

JESSIE. Who else am I going to be? I haven't got anyone else to be.

CAROLINE. Exactly, so you can leave all the difficult stuff to Dr Mitchell and me.

JESSIE. I thought you weren't my doctor.

CAROLINE. Yes. I've asked Charlie to look after you until you're eighteen – but I will still be helping on your case, I will give him advice because I've worked with you longer than everyone.

JESSIE. When can I get out?

CAROLINE. That'll be decided once you're eighteen.

JESSIE. Will they let me out?

CAROLINE. I hope so, I really do. (*Pause.*) Do you have any more questions?

JESSIE *shakes her head.*

Okay, then I'd better be going. It was lovely to speak to you again, Jessie.

JESSIE. I still think you're a witch.

CAROLINE. I know. (*Pause.*) Be good for Dr Charlie.

CAROLINE *exits.*

JESSIE *sits on the floor, hugging her knees to her chest.*

CHARLIE. Right. I think you should clear this mess up, shouldn't you?

JESSIE. …

CHARLIE. I said I think you should clear this mess up.

JESSIE. …

TOM. Jessie?

JESSIE. Tom can clear it up.

TOM. No. It's mess that you made.

JESSIE (*fighting back tears*). If you're keeping me here and you want to keep me, then you have to clear up my mess. That's the rules. That's the rules. You decided to keep me, I'm your pet and you have to clear up after me.

TOM. …

JESSIE. That's the rules… that's the rules, you can't change the rules.

TOM. Those aren't /

JESSIE. You said I could have a hamster as long as I cleaned up after it, I cleaned up after it, but it kept making a mess.

TOM. We don't /

JESSIE. And it didn't learn, and it kept making a mess. It didn't learn and so I threw it against the wall.

TOM. I said /

JESSIE. So throw me against the wall, smash my brains in, I don't want to be your pet any more.

JESSIE crosses to TOM *and grabs hold of his arms and pulls them around her throat.*

Throw me against the wall.

TOM. Let go.

JESSIE. Kill me. Kill me. Do it now. Smash my brains in.

TOM. Let go.

CHARLIE. …

TOM *eventually overpowers* JESSIE, *who passes out very quickly whilst* TOM *keeps her restrained.*

TOM. She's getting stronger.

TOM *picks her up and carries her back to her bed. He sedates her.*

Done. Sorry, Jessie.

He brushes her hair out of her eyes.

CHARLIE. She'll be fine in a few hours. Thanks for your help, Tom. Can you log 10:36 a.m.

TOM. Will do.

CHARLIE *exits*.

(*To* JESSIE.) Good girl. You did very well.

Scene Eleven

RACHEL *is at home. She finds the piece of paper with the drawing on it. It no longer horrifies her. She studies it.*

CHARLIE *enters*.

CHARLIE. I know I said I'd be back about /

RACHEL. It doesn't matter.

CHARLIE (*kissing her*). How have you been? How was work?

RACHEL. I didn't go. Couldn't face everyone. Everyone will know…

CHARLIE. There's nothing to be ashamed of.

RACHEL. I know. And I'm not. I shouldn't have told everyone. (*Pause*.) It's just… Oh, I don't know.

CHARLIE. Did you phone Erin?

RACHEL. Yeah. Sam's teething.

CHARLIE. Did she speak to you about the process, what it was like for her?

RACHEL. She said it was hard. But it was different, the twins were born, she's had Sam since.

CHARLIE. And we'll have a family too, soon.

RACHEL. It's taken us two years to get to here.

CHARLIE. But now we know we can.

RACHEL. What if we can't? What if this was our one go?

CHARLIE. It isn't. Of course it isn't. Don't be silly. We'll be right back here in a few months, having passed the screening and you'll be looking forward to making me run around after you.

RACHEL. How can you be sure?

CHARLIE. I can just feel it.

RACHEL. That's not very scientific.

CHARLIE. I'm not at work.

RACHEL. Will you come with me?

CHARLIE. Of course I will. I've booked all day Friday off. I'll drive us both there.

RACHEL. Don't they need you at work?

CHARLIE. I'm sure they'll survive without me for a few hours.

RACHEL. How was the girl today?

CHARLIE. We told her about her mum.

RACHEL. And?

CHARLIE. She struggled. There's lots of stuff that she doesn't know, that we don't know about her. Her mum evaded the authorities for so long that we've got no real picture of what her formative years were like, her early attachment patterns are a complete mystery and we have to infer any new attachment styles from her current behaviour. Jess's mother wasn't scanned, her grandparents managed to fiddle the paperwork somehow back when the authorities were a lot less rigorous. By the time her mental-health problems really kicked in she was already a teenager. She left the family home and went on the run.

RACHEL. Oh.

CHARLIE. We don't know much about what happened other than she fell pregnant with Jess. We don't think it was planned; it may have been rape.

RACHEL. That's awful.

CHARLIE. Life on the outside is.

RACHEL. But she didn't have a choice.

CHARLIE. Not really, no, her parents selfishly put her in that position.

RACHEL. It's sad.

CHARLIE. And Jessie should never have been born. Mistake after mistake after mistake.

RACHEL. But what about this? (*Holds up the paper*.)

CHARLIE. What about it?

RACHEL. It's good. For her age it's fantastic. She's never been taught. If she hadn't been born…

CHARLIE. I thought you hated it.

RACHEL. It's growing on me.

Scene Twelve

CAROLINE. You must get up before sunrise.

CHARLIE (*ignoring her*). I've got the footage from yesterday. This happened after you left.

CAROLINE. What?

CHARLIE. Jessie lost control at Tom…

CAROLINE. At Tom?

CHARLIE. Yes; watch here. She attempts to attack him…

CAROLINE. This isn't attacking behaviour.

CHARLIE. She was demanding that he kill her.

CAROLINE. What?!?

CHARLIE. He doesn't rise to the bait of course; but watch this… here he is. He applies pressure to her carotid arteries.

Now in a normal person… we'd be looking to escape, our eyes would be darting around, she maintains eye contact with me the entire time.

CAROLINE. She's asphyxiating, you can see.

CHARLIE. My point exactly; she's not afraid at all. She quietly accepts what is happening, her eye contact with me is an attempt to manipulate me into helping her.

CAROLINE. And did you?

CHARLIE. Of course not.

CAROLINE. …

CHARLIE. How much do we pay Tom?

CAROLINE. I have absolutely no idea.

CHARLIE. He incapacitated her within ten seconds, military training I suppose. His handling of the situation was quite masterful.

CAROLINE. …

CHARLIE. This footage is incredible.

CAROLINE. …

CHARLIE. I'm going to start the scanning tonight.

CAROLINE. She won't like that.

CHARLIE. She won't know. We're keeping her sedated, at least for the interim. See whether there's been any change in amygdala structure since you scanned her last.

CAROLINE. You can't keep her sedated!

CHARLIE. Why not?

CAROLINE. We were making progress with her. She hasn't needed restraining for the last few years.

CHARLIE. Do you know the recidivism rates for psychopathic behaviour?

CAROLINE. She isn't showing any psychopathic behaviour.

CHARLIE. That's because you haven't given her a chance to. We all saw how she went for you in the room…

CAROLINE. And she stopped herself. She was trying to elicit a fear response from me. She didn't actually attempt to touch me.

CHARLIE. Are you telling me that's normal behaviour?

CAROLINE. In that situation, for a twelve-year-old. Yes. You opened up a lot of unnecessary issues for her with the way that you handled the conversation.

CHARLIE. The way the conversation was handled is irrelevant; you can do all the behavioural observations that you want but what we actually need to do is scan her brain. That's the only way we can be sure of whether any sections are underdeveloped.

CAROLINE. The sedatives could affect her brain development, it could set her back years.

CHARLIE. That's a poor argument; there's been no scan of any of the major areas of interest since she was six.

CAROLINE. We're waiting for the uncinate fasciculus /

CHARLIE. Oh, come on, you've let her manipulate you and throw you off what you were employed to do.

CAROLINE. We scanned everywhere when she was younger and we will do so again, with her consent.

CHARLIE. …

CAROLINE. …

CHARLIE. I think you've become too attached.

CAROLINE (*incredulous*). Are you joking?

CHARLIE. You've started thinking of her as a girl.

CAROLINE. She *is* a girl.

Scene Thirteen

JESSIE *is pretending to be asleep.* TOM *enters.*

JESSIE. …

TOM. Hello. I can see that you're not asleep.

JESSIE. …

TOM. Would you like to do some drawing?

JESSIE. …

TOM. Are you going to ignore me for ever?

JESSIE. …

TOM. That's fine. Looks like it will be a quiet day at work for me.

JESSIE. …

TOM. I thought you should know, I've got permission to build a bird box near the skylight.

JESSIE. Did you?

TOM. Yes.

JESSIE. …

TOM. Hopefully you'll have a nice family of birds move in.

JESSIE *gets out of bed. She picks up her colouring pencils and pad and moves as far away from* TOM *as she can get.*

TOM *moves over to straighten her bed. He realises that she has wet the bed.*

Jessie?

JESSIE. …

TOM. The bed is wet.

JESSIE. …

TOM. Did you know that. (*Pause.*) Of course you knew that.

JESSIE. Clean it up.

TOM. Sorry?

JESSIE. You heard.

TOM. Someone is in a very bad mood, aren't they?

JESSIE. Clean it up.

TOM. Last time I checked, you weren't in charge.

JESSIE. …

TOM. …

JESSIE. Fine. Leave it.

> TOM *turns his back on* JESSIE *to sort out the bed. She takes a pencil and slowly moves towards him.*

TOM. I'm going to pretend you're not doing that.

> JESSIE *drops back to her drawing.*

I'm going to get some new sheets.

Scene Fourteen

TOM. You're working late.

CAROLINE. God, Tom. You're so bloody quiet.

TOM. Sorry. Force of habit. Is Charlie in?

CAROLINE. No, he's popped out.

TOM. Can you sign these?

> TOM *hands over a number of pieces of paper.*

CAROLINE. Sure. What are they?

TOM. Purchase orders.

CAROLINE. …

TOM. He's got a very different approach.

CAROLINE. Mmm?

TOM. It's a big adjustment, for Jess... for all of /

CAROLINE. What's this here?

TOM. For this evening.

CAROLINE. Right. I can't authorise this... it'll need to go through Charlie.

TOM. Okay.

CAROLINE. Did he say what they were for?

TOM. He wants to run some overnight tests; brain scans, doesn't want to disturb Jessie.

CAROLINE. Okay... thanks, Tom.

TOM. Shall I...

CAROLINE. I won't authorise this I'm afraid.

TOM. Okay... I can get the other stuff though?

CAROLINE. Yes. If you draw up a separate purchase order without the Xylodril I'll sign it.

TOM. You here for a while?

CAROLINE. Just catching up.

TOM. Okay. I'll pop back in a bit.

   TOM *exits*.

   CAROLINE *waits for him to leave. Checks the door and returns to the desk. She is looking for something. She opens up the computer.*

CHARLIE. Is there anything in particular you're looking for?

CAROLINE. Charlie! Is everyone sneaking up on me today?

CHARLIE. ...

CAROLINE. ...

CHARLIE. Was there anything in particular you were looking for?

CAROLINE. I was… the, uhm, there was something I wanted to raise with you.

CHARLIE. Yes.

CAROLINE. Tom wanted me to sign a purchase order.

CHARLIE. Right…

CAROLINE. Xylodril?

CHARLIE. What about it? You said that she had a phobia of brain scans.

CAROLINE. Yes but Xylodril? It's strong, and the side effects…

CHARLIE. Are minimal.

CAROLINE. For the rest of the planet perhaps. Hallucinations, nightmares, paranoia, agitation. For a single brain scan.

CHARLIE. That's why I've decided to do a full week of scans, get it over with. Minimise distress. I'm going to put together a full printout of her brain.

CAROLINE. Do you know how long that will take?

CHARLIE. At six hours a night, then we'll get a decent model together by the middle of next week.

CAROLINE. You're going to keep her awake for six hours a night?!

CHARLIE. She won't remember.

CAROLINE. Her body does. You're putting a twelve-year-old girl through MRI imaging for six hours a night for a week, without her consent. (*Pause*.) Have you even spoken with the medical team? What did Hattie Jackson say?

CHARLIE. Dr Jackson has said categorically that they're approved for therapeutic use; the whole paediatric team has approved them.

CAROLINE. What about addiction?

CHARLIE. Oh, come on, be serious.

CAROLINE. …

CHARLIE. She can't get addicted, we're controlling the dosage. We're a laboratory not a drug cartel.

CAROLINE. I don't think /

CHARLIE. The board are tired of hearing that we need more time, there hasn't been a significant breakthrough for a number of years. Why do you think they brought me in?

CAROLINE. They can't allow this.

CHARLIE. They can. And they have. Are you done looking through my computer now? I have work to do.

Scene Fifteen

CHARLE. I thought we could go away.

RACHEL. Away? Where?

CHARLIE. I don't know, I hadn't decided that far. I have the weekend off.

RACHEL. …

CHARLIE. You don't seem overly impressed with the idea.

RACHEL. I can't travel.

CHARLIE. Not at the moment, but after they lift the restrictions.

RACHEL. I think it takes longer than that, they'll have to reinstate / my passport.

CHARLIE. It takes a few hours at most.

RACHEL. I'm not going.

CHARLIE. We don't have to travel anywhere too far.

RACHEL. No. I'm not going to the termination centre.

CHARLIE. Rach...

RACHEL. I can't voluntarily walk through those doors.

CHARLIE. We knew this might happen, one-in-four chance. If
    you don't go, they will file an injunction. It'll take much
    longer /

RACHEL. I don't care. Let them file an injunction, I'm not
    setting foot /

CHARLIE. We'll get a fine.

RACHEL. Then we'll pay the fucking fine. If it's bothering you
    that much, I'll pay the fucking fine.

CHARLIE. It's a schedule-one condition.

RACHEL. I've been researching cystic fibrosis /

CHARLIE. I...

RACHEL. People lived with it. They treated it, there were
    drugs.

CHARLIE. Is this supposed to /

RACHEL. Where does it stop?

CHARLIE. What do you mean, where does it stop?

RACHEL. I was shortsighted when I was a kid, they corrected
    it at nursery – a specialist came in and lasered all of us that
    couldn't see properly. How long before that becomes a
    screened condition?

CHARLIE. You're sounding like some sort of conspiracy
    theorist.

RACHEL. People lived with cystic fibrosis all the time; and
    yes... they may have had shorter lives... but what about the

lives they did have. This baby could have your brains and my artistic ability and live until he or she was forty, die young and change the world…

CHARLIE. I can see you've thought about it a lot…

RACHEL. We could go away, there's another way… we could go.

CHARLIE. Rachel.

RACHEL. Why not? The three of us.

CHARLIE. For starters…

RACHEL. We could leave tonight.

CHARLIE. What you're /

RACHEL. Please? We might not get another chance.

CHARLIE. It's not an option.

RACHEL. Why not?

CHARLIE. The restrictions are there for a reason, if everyone /

RACHEL. Oh. Of course. Silly me.

CHARLIE. I'm not saying this isn't horrible, this is horrible; but running away is not the answer. This happens to thousands of couples, and thousands of couples have terminations every week.

RACHEL. I don't care about the thousands of couples, Charlie. This is happening to us. To me and to you.

CHARLIE. I appreciate that but /

RACHEL. But what? This is *our* baby.

CHARLIE. We always knew there was a chance that this would happen. We agreed how /

RACHEL. No. I agreed with you because I wanted you to stop talking, but I don't agree now. Our baby is too /

CHARLIE. It isn't a baby.

RACHEL. Put your hand here. (*Indicating her stomach.*) In there is a tiny beating heart, a tiny little person, half me, half you.

CHARLIE. That is not a baby; that is an unviable fetus with a schedule-one disorder, a disorder it had a one-in-four chance of contracting. No amount of emotional language will make it any different

RACHEL. No?

CHARLIE. …

RACHEL. …

CHARLIE. The quicker we go through with this, as horrible as it is, the quicker we can get our lives back to normal.

RACHEL. …

CHARLIE. We can start trying again straight away… if that's what you want. I know you're feeling emotional now, but there are a lot of hormones racing around your body, your brain / is probably all over the place.

RACHEL. Oh, just shut up.

CHARLIE. I'm just trying…

RACHEL. Not everything comes down to fucking science, Charlie; not everything can be solved by just examining the evidence – not everything I'm feeling is down to imbalances in my brain chemistry.

CHARLIE. Actually it is.

RACHEL. …

CHARLIE. Rach?

RACHEL. …

CHARLIE. Look, this is shit, this is really shit, for both of us. Once we've put this behind us, we can move on. I know it's hard, but I'm struggling to see why you have to make this so difficult for us both.

RACHEL (*sadly*). You really are, aren't you?

CHARLIE. Can we /

RACHEL. No. I'm done talking. (*Gets up to leave.*)

CHARLIE. Where are you going?

RACHEL. Out.

RACHEL *exits*.

Scene Sixteen

JESSIE *sits in the centre of the room. She is exhausted, she has dark circles under her eyes.*

TOM *enters*.

TOM. Hello.

JESSIE. …

TOM. Hello?

JESSIE. Hello, Tom.

TOM. No drawing today?

JESSIE. Not today.

TOM. Why not?

JESSIE. I can't make the pictures in my head.

TOM. You can do some tomorrow.

JESSIE. Maybe.

TOM. Come here. Let me do your hair, and you can take your pill.

JESSIE. Yes, Tom. (*Takes the pill.*)

TOM. No arguments?

JESSIE. Not today.

TOM. Right.

> JESSIE *crosses to him and sits in front of him. He plaits her hair.*

JESSIE. Tom?

TOM. Yes.

JESSIE. Am I going to die?

TOM. …

JESSIE. Tom?

TOM. We're all going to die, Jess.

JESSIE. Even you?

TOM. Even me.

JESSIE. You're not allowed, you're the only thing in my room that I like.

TOM. Don't be silly.

JESSIE. …

TOM. Besides, I'm not in your room all the time. You must like other things.

JESSIE. I don't, not really. But when you're not in my room, I have my picture of you.

TOM. What picture?

JESSIE. I draw it in my head until you come back.

TOM. …

JESSIE. But today I couldn't draw it. My head stopped working.

TOM. …

JESSIE. …

TOM. What's the matter?

JESSIE (*panicking*). I couldn't draw it. Tom, I couldn't draw it.

TOM. Shhhh.

JESSIE (*overwhelmed*). I couldn't draw you, I couldn't remember what your face looked like.

TOM. It looks like this… (*Smiles at her.*) See?

JESSIE. But I've never forgotten your face before and I was scared.

TOM. …

JESSIE. What if you didn't come back? What if I forgot you for ever. I don't want to be me if I can't remember you.

TOM. I'm not going anywhere, your room is always a mess, there's always lots for me to do. (*Finishes her hair.*) Now look, you're being silly and you're getting your eyes all puffy.

TOM *makes a game of wiping her tears away.*

JESSIE. Can I touch your face?

TOM. What?

JESSIE. I'm not allowed to, I know… but I think if I did, then I would remember it better.

TOM (*looking at the mirror*). No sudden movements.

JESSIE. Promise.

JESSIE *places her hands on* TOM*'s face. She closes her eyes and feels across his features. She smiles.*

Thank you.

Scene Seventeen

JESSIE *is sitting*. CHARLIE *enters*. TOM *watches from the side*.

CHARLIE. I have something for you.

JESSIE. What?

CHARLIE. It's very old, but it's yours.

CHARLIE *offers a book to* JESSIE, *who takes it hesitantly.*

JESSIE. What is it?

CHARLIE. Drawings.

JESSIE. Drawings?

JESSIE *opens the book and begins to look through the pictures.*

CHARLIE. Your mum did them, when you were still with her and really little; most of the drawings are of you. I have been waiting for the right time to give it to you.

JESSIE. This is me here?

CHARLIE. Yes.

JESSIE. And this is my real mother?

CHARLIE. Yes. Her name was Grace.

JESSIE. I know. Grace. That's pretty. She's very pretty.

CHARLIE. Yes she is.

JESSIE (*solemnly*). This is the most important thing I have ever had. Can I keep it?

CHARLIE. Of course; it's yours.

JESSIE. It is the best thing I have ever had. Apart from Tom.

CHARLIE. I thought you could put your sketches in there too, so you can show Tom.

JESSIE. I don't want to draw in it until I am better.

CHARLIE. You're pretty good already.

JESSIE. No. When I am better. When you've cured me.

CHARLIE. ...

JESSIE. Dr Charlie?

CHARLIE. Yes.

JESSIE (*whispering*). If I am good, can I go and live with Tom?

CHARLIE. What?

JESSIE. If I am good. Can I live with Tom? If I promise to be good. Promise not to be silly and not try to kiss him. If I keep everything tidy?

CHARLIE. Why do you want to go and live with Tom?

JESSIE. Because Tom always has to come here. But if I lived with him. Then he wouldn't always have to come here. It would be easier. You could come and visit.

CHARLIE. What do you think Tom would say?

JESSIE. I don't think he would be allowed.

CHARLIE. No, he wouldn't.

JESSIE. But you make the decisions, so you could make the decision.

CHARLIE. Some of them.

JESSIE. So if you told him, he would have to, wouldn't he?

CHARLIE. No.

JESSIE. Can you make him live here?

CHARLIE. No.

JESSIE (*suddenly aggressive*). Make him! I want Tom to live here with me.

CHARLIE. Sit down.

JESSIE. No! You think you're in charge, but you're not in charge. I'm in charge.

JESSIE picks up a pencil from underneath her pillow. She brandishes it like a weapon.

CHARLIE. I'm not scared of you.

JESSIE. …

CHARLIE. That might work on other people, but it won't work on me.

JESSIE (*moving closer*). It does.

CHARLIE. It doesn't.

They lock gazes. JESSIE moves the pencil into line with CHARLIE's eye. She moves it closer and closer. TOM stands up ready to intervene but CHARLIE indicates that he is fine.

JESSIE. …

CHARLIE. I'm appreciating the theatrics, Jessica, but you should stop.

JESSIE. Make me.

CHARLIE. You having fun?

JESSIE. No. This isn't fun, this is serious.

CHARLIE. No?

JESSIE. Make me stop then. Make me. MAKE ME.

CHARLIE. I can make Tom never be in your room again.

JESSIE drops the pencil.

JESSIE. …

CHARLIE. That's much better.

JESSIE. I thought you were nice.

CHARLIE. I thought you were nice too. Sometimes we are.

JESSIE. ...

CHARLIE. Are you scared of me?

JESSIE. No.

CHARLIE *suddenly screams in her face*. JESSIE *doesn't blink*. CHARLIE *nods*.

TOM. Charlie, what are you doing?

CHARLIE. A short informal test.

TOM. You can't just shout in her face.

CHARLIE. Mark it as 14:47.

CHARLIE *exits*.

TOM. Are you okay, Jessie?

JESSIE. I have a new book! Do you want to see in my new book? It belonged to my mum, her name was Grace. She was very pretty, there's lots of pictures of me too from when I was a baby. Do you want to see?

TOM (*bemused*). Okay.

JESSIE. You can't touch it though.

TOM. Okay.

JESSIE. Unless I tell you that you can. Because it is mine.

TOM (*to* JESSIE). Everything okay with Dr Charlie?

JESSIE. I don't like him today.

Scene Eighteen

RACHEL *is standing and waiting. We don't know what for. She takes out her mobile phone and thinks about texting. She decides against it. She places it on the floor along with her purse and bag.*

A hear the sound of a car pulling up. Headlights. She leaves her phone, purse and bag, and exits. The car drives away.

Scene Nineteen

CHARLIE. …

CAROLINE. You okay? You look like death.

CHARLIE. Rachel didn't come home last night.

CAROLINE. What?!

CHARLIE. I think she's gone to Erin's, to her sister's house, but nobody is picking up my calls.

CAROLINE. …

CHARLIE. She's now in breach of a termination order…

CAROLINE. Do you want to go home? I can cover the project. I managed for nine years without your help, I'm sure I could cover it for another day.

CHARLIE. I'm fine. She'll get in touch when she's calmed down…

CAROLINE. …

Long pause.

CHARLIE. I've asked permission to do investigative surgery on the uncinate fasciculus.

CAROLINE. Right…

CHARLIE. The ethics council has provisionally approved it.

CAROLINE. No.

CHARLIE. I'm sorry?

CAROLINE. I said no. You can't go poking around inside her brain /

CHARLIE. I thought you might have objections.

CAROLINE. I do.

CHARLIE. She threatened to push a pencil through my eye.

CAROLINE. And did she actually do it?

CHARLIE. Of course not.

CAROLINE. You're working on a scan and a hunch that's leading us down a very dangerous road. You've showed up to work in this state, have you even slept?

CHARLIE. We've got nine years of your meticulous observation showing pretty much nothing. Only since I began actually testing her have we seen any...

CAROLINE. And what have we seen, Charlie? What evidence have you actually amassed in the two days you've turned her world inside out?

CHARLIE. She has delayed fear responses, she is manipulative, she's violent.

CAROLINE. She's also been kept in a room for the last nine years, she's had no play friends, since she was four.

CHARLIE. After she punched another child.

CAROLINE. Yes, she hit another child; but she was *four* – that's what four-year-olds do. And yes she's manipulative... but she's a twelve-year-old girl. She might be violent, but she hasn't actually attacked anyone.

CHARLIE. Tom?

CAROLINE. Emotional containment, Charlie. She knows full well that she can't hurt Tom, she isn't capable.

CHARLIE. She enjoys the violence.

CAROLINE. There is nothing unusual in her behaviour that can't be explained by someone who has read a pamphlet about basic psychology.

CHARLIE. That is your opinion. I respectfully disagree.

CAROLINE. I will get this rescinded. You can't do this, it's completely immoral.

CHARLIE. Oh, for God's sake, it's exploratory surgery.

CAROLINE. Where does it stop? When will you stop poking and prodding her? You haven't found anything conclusive so far, will you just keep looking, keep poking new parts of the brain /

CHARLIE. I'll stop when we have a conclusive answer, this is what she's here for. Experimentation.

CAROLINE. Yesterday your plan was two weeks' worth of brain scans, today it's surgery.

CHARLIE. Because /

CAROLINE. Your plans are continually changing.

CAROLINE *goes to pack up her things.*

CHARLIE. Where are you going?

CAROLINE. I'm going to speak to Professor Cass about the jeopardy you're putting this project under.

CAROLINE *storms out as* TOM *comes in.*

TOM. Hi... oh, sorry. I didn't mean to interrupt.

CHARLIE. What can I do for you?

TOM. I'm doing the night shift. I have to sort out the rota for next week. Jessie seems unsettled.

CHARLIE. That's to be expected.

TOM. She's been very spaced out, she's finding drawing difficult.

CHARLIE. Lethargy is a side effect.

TOM. She's complained of constipation.

CHARLIE. That's temporary.

TOM. And /

CHARLIE. Tom! (*Pause.*) It's to be expected.

TOM (*looking at the scan*). Is this her brain?

CHARLIE. Yes.

TOM. So… can you cure it? She keeps asking about being cured; I don't know what to tell her.

CHARLIE. Tell her whatever keeps her happiest and most settled.

TOM. Is it even a curable condition?

Pause.

CHARLIE. I've got things to do before tonight's session.

Scene Twenty

TOM. I didn't realise we were due a night visit?

CAROLINE. I need to see Jessie.

TOM. She's not awake. She's been asleep since ten o'clock.

CAROLINE. Has Charlie gone?

TOM. Yes.

CAROLINE. Will he be back?

TOM. He's going to come back just before the handover tomorrow.

CAROLINE. He's planning surgery on her.

TOM. What?!

CAROLINE. I've come to get her out.

TOM. You can't take her out!

CAROLINE. It's the only thing I can do.

TOM. She hasn't been out of here since she was three, it won't…

CAROLINE. Do you think there's anything wrong with her, Tom? Anything at all?

TOM. She's a psychopath.

CAROLINE. Is she?

TOM. …

CAROLINE. I'm asking you…

TOM. Not really my place to say. You're the doctors. I just look after her.

CAROLINE. And you've looked after her for six years; so your opinion is just as good as mine. Do you think she's a psychopath?

TOM. I don't know.

CAROLINE. Neither do I. I'd like to think she isn't; and I'd like to think that I'm right about that. The way she behaves with you shows genuine compassion. She asks after you when you're not in.

TOM. I know.

CAROLINE. I've looked at the evidence, I've looked at the bloody brain scans and it doesn't tell me anything. All I see in there is a little girl.

TOM. What will the surgery do?

CAROLINE. At the moment it's exploratory; but God knows what else he has up his sleeves.

TOM. Will it hurt her?

CAROLINE. Perhaps. I don't know…

TOM. Where can you take her?

CAROLINE. At the moment anywhere is preferable to here.

TOM. …

CAROLINE. …

TOM. I should call the police.

CAROLINE. …

TOM. She's a potential danger to the people out there.

CAROLINE. She's a child.

TOM. I know that.

CAROLINE. A child is a child is a child.

TOM. But Jessie /

CAROLINE. But Jessie what? She made it into the world under absolutely horrific circumstances and we've tried to encourage her towards becoming a caring and /

TOM. That's not how Charlie / sees it.

CAROLINE. We've known her, watched her grow. We see her as she is.

TOM. She'll be safer here with me than out there.

CAROLINE. You can't protect her from him. You've got a family to support.

TOM. Jessie is part of my family.

CAROLINE. Then let her come with me. She's my family too. I'll take care of her.

TOM. You wouldn't be able to handle her. She won't cope well with the changes; I don't know if she's ready…

CAROLINE. If the surgeries happen there will be more drugs, she'll be more unpredictable. Eventually she'll do something to someone, probably Charlie – and he will be forced to have her destroyed.

TOM. …

CAROLINE (*showing him the sedatives*). You can tell everyone that I surprised you – that you had no idea. You'll wake up and be none the wiser; they won't have anything on you.

TOM. What if she attacks someone when she's outside?

CAROLINE. I'm hoping that she won't; praying, even. I don't have long.

TOM. Wait. (*Goes into his wallet.*) Give her this. (*Pause.*) It's me and my kids; she doesn't have anything.

Scene Twenty-One

JESSIE *is sleeping. She is dreaming.*

CAROLINE. Jessie? (*Pause.*) Jessie? Jessie.

    CAROLINE *crosses to where* JESSIE *is sleeping.*

    Jessie. It's time to wake up. We need to go.

JESSIE. Huh?

CAROLINE. We need to go. Come on.

    CAROLINE *puts her hand on* JESSIE*'s shoulder to shake her awake.*

JESSIE. Tom?

CAROLINE. No. Jessie, it's me. It's Dr Caroline.

JESSIE. You woke me up.

CAROLINE. I'm sorry. You need to listen to me very carefully.

JESSIE. Okay.

CAROLINE. I need you to come with me. Quietly.

JESSIE. Where?

CAROLINE. I'll answer all of your questions soon, but we need to go.

JESSIE. Can I bring my pencils?

CAROLINE. Of course you can; but we need to go quickly.

JESSIE. Why? Where are we going? Are we going outside?

CAROLINE. Yes.

JESSIE. I'm not going outside without Tom.

CAROLINE. He said that you should be a good girl and do exactly what I say.

JESSIE. Why didn't he come and get me?

CAROLINE. He sent me instead.

JESSIE. You're lying. Your voice is doing that thing when people lie. Where's Tom?

CAROLINE. He's waiting outside.

JESSIE. TOM! You're lying. TOM!

CAROLINE. You need to be quiet.

CAROLINE *touches* JESSIE *on the shoulder.*

JESSIE. TOM!!! Don't touch me.

CAROLINE. We need to go.

JESSIE. TOM! TOM!

CAROLINE *tries to put her hand over* JESSIE's *mouth. There there is a scuffle and* CAROLINE *falls to the floor.*

You're not Tom. TOM! TOM! TOM! TOM! I need you! TOM, I did something bad! Tom! I did something. Tom!

JESSIE *looks at the open door. She crosses to it.*

Tom? Tom… Tom?… Tom?

JESSIE *contemplates leaving. She goes to the door. She comes back. She goes to the door and then makes up her mind and sits on her bed.*

Scene Twenty-Two

CHARLIE *and* TOM *sit opposite sides of the desk.*

CHARLIE. You're telling me you didn't see her?

TOM. No I'm saying I didn't expect to be sedated, I've known her for years. Why would she do something like that? I don't see what this has got to do with me.

CHARLIE. I'm struggling to see how a sixty-five-year-old woman managed to knock you unconscious without you having time to react or alert anyone.

TOM. Maybe it was a bad day. We're all allowed off-days.

CHARLIE. You know you'll be in a bad place if you lie.

TOM. It's a good job I'm not lying then.

CHARLIE. …

TOM. …

CHARLIE. I've been summoned to give evidence. They want to know what sort of security breach allowed a registered psychopath access to the outside world.

TOM. She didn't leave.

CHARLIE. But she could've done. The door was open until I came in.

TOM. It wasn't unprovoked; something happened between the two of them.

CHARLIE. Caroline got lucky. If I hadn't decided on an early start anything could've happened.

TOM. Jessie didn't do anything. She just sat on her bed.

CHARLIE. She committed an act of violence.

TOM. She was confused. Disorientated.

CHARLIE. She didn't try and get help. She enjoyed the blood.

TOM. Bollocks.

CHARLIE. She watched as Caroline bled.

TOM. She zoned out, she does that!

CHARLIE. Either way… it's a tough argument to make.

TOM. I'll make it. You, all of you… you've poked her and prodded her, and fucked about with her head so much she doesn't know whether she's coming or going. Caroline arrives in the middle of the night and talks to her about God knows what, something happens that we can't really see and suddenly it's conclusive proof she's a psychopath.

CHARLIE. That's great, Tom, let me know when you get your PhD in Neuroscience.

TOM *goes to say something. Thinks better of it.*

TOM. If anything happens to her…

CHARLIE. If anything happens to her it'll be because of last night's monumental fuck-up.

TOM *pauses at the door.*

TOM. What are her chances?

CHARLIE. It's fifty-fifty. But there's a strong case for the prosecution.

TOM. And if they agree, then how exactly would it…

CHARLIE. Lethal injection.

TOM. …

CHARLIE. Caroline has taken full responsibility, there are lots of extenuating circumstances. I should warn you that if Caroline makes contact with you, you are to obliged to inform us. Any attempt to collude with her will be seen as gross misconduct.

TOM. …

CHARLIE. On a purely academic note she's much more use to this project alive than she is dead. So I will be supporting the case for the defence. The irony of this entire situation is that Caroline's actions have put Jessie's life in question.

Scene Twenty-Three

JESSIE *is sitting on her bed. She is subdued.* TOM *enters*

JESSIE. Tom! (*Runs to hug him. Changes her mind and turns her back on him.*) I thought you were gone. You always come in the mornings. I thought you were gone for ever.

TOM. I wouldn't go without saying goodbye. I've just had things to do.

JESSIE. Am I in trouble?

TOM. Lots of people are talking about you.

JESSIE. Really?

TOM. Yes. Important people, there's a big meeting about you.

JESSIE. Did you tell them what I said?

TOM. I have. I've told everyone what you said.

JESSIE. Did you tell them that I didn't leave?

TOM. I did.

JESSIE. Even though the door was open.

TOM. I did.

JESSIE. They might listen to you if you tell them I wasn't bad.

TOM. They might.

JESSIE. Tom?

TOM. Yes.

JESSIE. I'm sad.

TOM. Why?

JESSIE. I thought if I was good that they would let me live with you. But this looks like I was bad, doesn't it. The witch is going to tell them that I hit her really hard, but I didn't hit her *that* hard. I didn't mean to. And I called for you.

TOM. I know that.

JESSIE. Can you tell everyone it was her fault?

TOM. She is already telling everyone that it's her fault; she's got into a lot of trouble for trying to take you out.

JESSIE. Oh. Good. Because if Dr Caroline was bad for taking me out, then me staying here can only be a good thing, can't it? Because that's the opposite of what she asked me to do. I've been good. (*Smiles.*)

TOM. It's a bit more complicated than that.

JESSIE (*worried*). Did I get you in trouble?

TOM. No, I'm not in trouble.

JESSIE. That's good. (*Pause.*) I have something for you.

TOM. …

JESSIE. I did you a drawing for your house.

> JESSIE *gets a drawing of her and* TOM *out from under her bed*.

> This is me here.

TOM. …

JESSIE. And this is you… I did it big because I thought you might be able to keep it.

TOM. …

JESSIE. Will you be allowed to keep it?

TOM. It's very good.

JESSIE. It's my best drawing. I will tell them it's just for you and nobody else. I can do the mirror people other drawings, this one is just for you.

TOM. I have nothing to give you.

JESSIE. I don't want anything, as long as you keep coming back I can keep doing you drawings.

TOM *thinks for a second. He gives* JESSIE *a kiss on the forehead.*

She is shocked. She breaks into a huge smile.

Once they finish talking about how good I was they'll probably let me come and see this be put up in your house, won't they? If I ask them nicely? I can ask them nicely.

TOM. Maybe.

Scene Twenty-Four

CHARLIE. They've given me a six-month window of intensive testing in which to make the decision. They think that she presents a risk to the public; a gross oversight like the one that we just had could leave us all vulnerable to attack.

TOM. But she didn't leave.

CHARLIE. They want her strongly sedated… Indefinitely. They're happy for us to bring her out of sedation in order to carry out experiments provided we make an application in writing and ensure adequate risk assessments… but other than that, they want her immobile.

TOM. In a coma?

CHARLIE. No. Conscious; paralysed from the neck down with muscle relaxants. We still need to run stimuli tests to check brain-functioning.

TOM. You can't keep her paralysed!

CHARLIE. We don't have a choice, thanks to Caroline they have issued an order; you have a problem, take it up with them.

TOM. What about her drawing?

CHARLIE (*nonplussed*). She won't be able to do any. (*Pause.*) We have enough information about her behaviours. I have more important questions now and we don't need her to be moving in order to establish answers; thus the risk is reduced.

TOM. You don't have any problems with this?

CHARLIE. I have a job to do, Tom… this makes my job easier. In a perfect world we wouldn't have to go through this rigmarole, they haven't left me with any choice. We need to keep her under sedation until we can equip a long-term paediatric ward with the necessary equipment. I would advise you, if you want to keep your job that is, to take Jessie her meds and prepare her for the evening session. Now if you can get on with what you're paid for, so can I.

Scene Twenty-Five

JESSIE *waits in her room. She lying on her back, drawing a bird in the skylight.*

JESSIE. Careful. If you're too loud the bird will fly off. Look. (*Points.*)

TOM. The hawk.

JESSIE. He came back this morning, I think he likes me.

TOM. I've got something exciting to tell you!

JESSIE. What?!

TOM. Put the drawings down for a second.

JESSIE. What? What is it?

TOM. The people behind the mirror have been talking about you.

JESSIE. Am I in trouble?

TOM. No. Because you didn't run off when you could've… they decided that you'd been good, you've been really good.

JESSIE. …

TOM. So well done, you.

JESSIE. Are you lying to me, Tom?

TOM. When have I ever lied to you?

JESSIE. That's true. You have never lied before.

TOM. They've said that you can come out with me. Tomorrow.

JESSIE (*amazed*). Really!?!

TOM. Yes. I got permission from Dr Charlie.

JESSIE. Wow.

TOM. And… they also said that you could come and live with me. If you wanted.

JESSIE. …

TOM. But after tomorrow. They need to run some final tests today so I've got to give you a sedative.

JESSIE. The needles?

TOM. Yes.

JESSIE. I don't like the needles.

TOM. I know… but once.

JESSIE. This is the best day ever! Do I need to pack?

TOM. We can do it tomorrow. What do you want to eat?

JESSIE. I'm too excited to eat.

TOM. I can give you the sedative now. You'll be asleep until tomorrow.

JESSIE. Okay! What time will I wake up tomorrow.

TOM. I don't know. It depends how long they want to do the tests and how much I give you.

JESSIE. Can I wake up in the afternoon?

TOM. I don't know if I can be that accurate.

JESSIE. What will we do at your house, Tom?

TOM. We can do whatever you like.

JESSIE. I want to play outside in the sunshine. I like the sunshine. Will I have to sleep on the floor?

TOM. No. We've got a special bedroom ready for you.

JESSIE. This is the best day of all for ever. (*Pause*.) Will you be there when I wake up.

TOM. Of course I will.

JESSIE. Good, because I don't know where your house is. You'll have to take me because I would get lost on my own.

TOM. We won't expect you to find it yourself.

JESSIE. I don't think I even could.

TOM. Are you ready? (*Indicates the needle*.)

JESSIE. I suppose.

TOM (*injecting her*). There's a good girl...

JESSIE. Can I draw things?

TOM. Of course, you can... you're one of the best artists in the world I think.

JESSIE. That's the nicest thing anyone has ever said to me. (*Pause*.) Tom, what time are we going to your house? We can go after I sleep, can't we, and you won't go without me? I won't miss it, will I? What will we tell people? Because people will ask... people will say that's Tom's cat, and I will say no... I will say I'm a person that I'm... I will say... no. I'm not Tom's cat... I'm... his –

The lights fade to black.

The End.

A Nick Hern Book

Tomcat first published in Great Britain in 2015 as a paperback original by Nick Hern Books Limited, The Glasshouse, 49a Goldhawk Road, London W12 8QP, in association with Papatango and Southwark Playhouse, London

Tomcat copyright © 2015 James Rushbrooke

James Rushbrooke has asserted his right to be identified as the author of this work

Cover image by Rebecca Pitt

Designed and typeset by Nick Hern Books, London
Printed in the UK by Mimeo Ltd, Huntingdon, Cambridgeshire PE29 6XX

A CIP catalogue record for this book is available from the British Library

ISBN 978 1 84842 516 3

Woodland CARBON
www.woodlandcarbon.co.uk
NICK HERN BOOKS
Printed on Carbon Captured paper